THIS COULD BE OUR FUTURE

WH
ALLEN

THIS COULD BE OUR FUTURE

A MANIFESTO FOR A

MORE GENEROUS WORLD

YANCEY STRICKLER

1 3 5 7 9 10 8 6 4 2

WH Allen, an imprint of Ebury Publishing,
20 Vauxhall Bridge Road,
London SW1V 2SA

WH Allen is part of the Penguin Random House group of companies
whose addresses can be found at global.penguinrandomhouse.com

Penguin
Random House
UK

First published in the United States by Viking in 2019
First published in the United Kingdom by WH Allen in 2019

www.penguin.co.uk

A CIP catalogue record for this book is available from the British Library

ISBN 9780753552834

Grateful acknowledgment is made to the following:
Page 66: Photo courtesy of Tim Rohan and Stan Connors.
Page 88: Harvard Business Review October 2015 cover reprinted
with permission of Harvard Business Publishing.
Page 130: Photo courtesy of Kohei Nishida.
Bentoism and Bento images created by Yancey Strickler
with design support from Laurel Schwulst.
All other images courtesy of the author.

Printed and bound in Great Britain by Clays Ltd, Elcograf S.p.A.

Penguin Random House is committed to a sustainable future for
our business, our readers and our planet. This book is made
from Forest Stewardship Council® certified paper.

MIX
Paper from
responsible sources
FSC
www.fsc.org   FSC® C018179

For Koji, and the rest of Future Us

CONTENTS

IT STARTED WITH A HEADLINE.

It was fall. I was walking in New York City with my wife and son. I saw it out of the corner of my eye.

"PLA to be world-class force by 2050," read the front page of *China Daily*. Beneath the headline was a picture of President Xi Jinping and a row of People's Liberation Army soldiers.

The year leapt out: 2050. Distant, but not too distant. Thirty-three years away from that moment. *I'll probably still be alive then.*

A thought hit me. While China was planning for 2050, my own country, the United States, couldn't agree whether to pay that month's bills.

Where should we be in 2050?

I couldn't stop thinking about this.

■ ■ ■ ■

The book in your hands is an answer to that question. Not *the* answer, *an* answer. But before we get to 2050, first we need to know where we are right now.

Today the world is dominated by an idea I call "financial maximization." The belief that in any decision, the right choice is whichever option makes the most money. This is the default setting that runs much of our world.

In business, economics, and finance, the importance of financial growth is as fundamental as it gets. The whole point of having money is to make more of it.

But the force of financial maximization that's emerged in recent decades is something different. It's bigger and more powerful than it's been before. The drive to financially maximize has come to dominate many of our organizations, our institutions, and even our dreams. Money is becoming all that matters.

Michael Lewis, author of *Moneyball* and *The Big Short*, wrote a book called *Liar's Poker* about his experience working on Wall Street right at the moment financial maximization took off in the 1980s. Lewis writes that his fellow traders "assume that anything that enables them to get rich must also be good for the world." It didn't matter whether their actions created jobs or destroyed them. All that mattered was that they were making lots of money doing it.

This is what financial maximization has done to society on a mass scale. It has convinced us that in any decision, the correct choice is whatever option makes the most money, with no concept of "good" or "bad" beyond that. Good and bad are too irrational for financial maximization's Terminator-like thinking. It only cares whether there's "less" or "more." And it always wants more.

As financial maximization has grown, its influence has breached the riverbanks of finance. In a widening array of areas, we're increasingly wired to believe that the right answer is whatever produces the greatest financial return. Other values come second, or not at all.

The focus on financial growth isn't wrong. Without financial security, life spans for people and organizations decrease. That's bad. Money is important. It's just not the *only* form of value we should protect and grow.

Financial maximization has trapped us with three assumptions: (1) that the point of life is to maximize financial wealth, (2) that we're individuals trapped in an adversarial world, and (3) that this situation is inevitable and eternal.

We see these ideas as truths. They're not. They're ideas that previous generations proposed and accepted. They're assumptions that separate us, keep us powerless, and limit our imagination for the future. They're ideas that we must reexamine if we want to go somewhere new.

■ ■ ■

This book is about a simple idea.

That a world of scarcity can become a world of abundance if we accept a broader definition of value.

We recognize that there are many valuable things in life—love, community, safety, knowledge, and faith, to name just a few. But we allow just one value—money—to dominate everything else. Our potential for a more generous, moral, or fair society is limited by the dominance of money as the be-all and end-all. It puts a ceiling on what we can be.

Until very recently, conversations like this were on the fringes of society. But in recent years they've become more mainstream. In 2019, Fox News host Tucker Carlson sharply questioned financial maximization during a fifteen-minute monologue on his prime-time show. He said:

> At some point, Donald Trump will be gone. The rest of us will be gone, too. The country will remain. What kind of country will it be then? How do we want our grandchildren to live? These are the only questions that matter.
>
> The answer used to be obvious. The overriding goal for America was more prosperity, meaning cheaper consumer goods. But is that still true? Does anyone still believe that cheaper iPhones or more Amazon deliveries of plastic garbage from China are going to make us happy? They haven't so far. A lot of Americans are drowning in stuff. And yet drug addiction and suicide are depopulating large parts of the country. Anyone who thinks the health of a nation can be summed up in GDP is an idiot . . .
>
> We are ruled by mercenaries who feel no long-term obligation to the people they rule. They're day traders. Substitute teachers. They're just passing through. They have no skin in

this game, and it shows. They can't solve our problems. They don't even bother to understand our problems . . .

For our ruling class, more investment banking is always the answer. They teach us it's more virtuous to devote your life to some soulless corporation than it is to raise your own kids. . . .

Market capitalism is not a religion. Market capitalism is a tool, like a staple gun or a toaster. You'd have to be a fool to worship it. Our system was created by human beings for the benefit of human beings. We do not exist to serve markets. Just the opposite. Any economic system that weakens and destroys families is not worth having. A system like that is the enemy of a healthy society.

Across the political spectrum, people can feel that financial maximization has taken us off course.

This book proposes what we should do instead: end financial maximization's reign as the primary driver of human activity by expanding our idea of value.

The goal isn't to get rid of money. It's not to eradicate greed. It's not anti-profits, either. The goal is a world where values like community, knowledge, purpose, fairness, security, tradition, and the needs of the future also have a rational say in the big and daily decisions we face. Not just whichever choice makes the most money.

I believe that future is possible. And I believe it can be here faster than we think. By 2050 we can expand our idea of rational value beyond financial maximization, and grow value in new ways.

The year 2050 is more than a round number in a newspaper headline. It's a generation from now. Thirty years away from this moment. Thirty years is the right timescale to think about significant change.

Thirty years is how long it took to create the internet. Thirty years is how long it took to get from exercise not being a thing to gyms and yoga studios being almost everywhere. Thirty years is how long it took most of the population to quit smoking. The law of compounding interest says a small amount of change adds up each year, gaining momentum as it grows.

Thirty years from now—2050—will be the first time society will be led by the Millennial and Z generations. Two groups notable in many ways, including for being the first to grow up after the internet. These generations show a strong dissatisfaction with the world they're inheriting. In a 2014 poll by Harvard's Institute of Politics, just 19 percent of Americans between the ages of nineteen and twenty-nine called themselves capitalists, and less than half said they supported capitalism.

The people in these generations have a tremendous opportunity—I would even say responsibility—to think carefully about where they want to lead us. Thirty years is not that far away. It will be here faster than we think.

Three centuries ago, people lived as aristocrats or subjects. The idea of a person as an individual with rights was like the self-driving car of 2016: cool in theory, but far from an everyday reality. The idea that the rich would willfully share power was unthinkable. You had to petition the House of Lords to start a company. Children were expected to work long hours of hard labor.

Then new ideas developed and spread for how the world could work. The French Revolution, the Declaration of Independence, Adam Smith, Karl Marx, the Beatles, hip-hop, and *Star Trek: The Next Generation* in the blink of an eye. It was a very different world and it wasn't that long ago.

Where should the 2050 generations lead us? I believe that expanding our definition of value is the goal to work toward.

There is unlimited potential to increase the amount of fairness, mastery, purpose, community, knowledge, family, faith, tradition, and sustainability in our world if we accept a broader idea of value. We can use the skills and tools we've developed for financial growth to support and protect a wider value spectrum. This is the evolutionary path that lets us keep growing without tearing it all down.

■ ■ ■ ■

Who am I to be telling you all of this?

We'll get to my story in a minute. But you should know that I'm not an economist or historian. I'm a civilian in many of the areas we'll explore. This book isn't trying to make an airtight legal argument, nor does it. As the title says, the book is a manifesto. An argument for a new way to see based on data, historical events, and personal experiences.

The book is split into two parts.

The first half explores how we got to now, including where financial maximization came from and how it reshaped our neighborhoods, our politics, and even the movies and the mall.

The second half proposes a new way to think about value. I explain how the pop star Adele, the three-point shot, and the history of medicine demonstrate what happens when we discover new approaches to value. And how a Japanese lunch box might be the secret to our escape. Following the last chapter, the Appendix and an extensive Notes section go deeper into the ideas and thought processes behind the book, provide sources for the book's facts and figures, and share a reading list and next steps.

My ultimate hope for this book is that someone—maybe it's you—finds these ideas worth engaging with and building on. And from that collaboration between your ideas, my ideas, and the many shoulders these ideas stand on, a better way of living becomes possible, and future generations can live in a world where value is better understood.

This is a big idea. But by the end of this book, I hope to convince you that it's also an achievable idea. If you have a destination, it's amazing how far you can go.

THIS COULD BE OUR FUTURE

PART ONE

CHAPTER ONE

A SIMPLE IDEA

NARRATORS BRING THEIR OWN STORY. YOU MIGHT AS WELL know mine from the start.

I was born in 1978 in southwest Virginia. My mother was a secretary at a local college. My father was a traveling waterbed salesman and a musician.

When I was three, they divorced. My mom remarried a few years later. She and I moved to a farm in a place nearby called Clover Hollow. That's where I grew up.

My mother, stepfather, and I were evangelical Christians. We went to churches where people danced in the aisles and spoke in tongues. Our pastors preached about living in service to God, loving one another, and the wickedness of the world around us. Until sixth grade, I went to a Christian school where Bible study was part of the daily schedule.

Most people were like this where I grew up. Even so, I didn't fit in. I didn't play football. I was one of the few boys who went to school on the first day of hunting season. I was bullied. On the school bus boys put gum in my hair, threw a can of Coke at me, and spit Skoal on me. I got called homophobic slurs so often I wondered if I was gay and didn't know it. Those were hard years.

But I was ambitious. My dream was to be a writer. After graduating from college I moved to New York to pursue it. I'd saved $2,500 from working as the night clerk at a motel and doing tech support at my school.

And somehow, I made it. I got a low-paying but great job turning news stories into tiny capsule news briefs for radio stations before getting laid off (more on that later). I got my first paycheck from writing: $75 for a record review in *The Village Voice*. I was far from the best or best-known music critic, but I carved out a niche doing it for almost a decade. My dream came true.

And then Kickstarter happened.

Perry Chen first had the idea for Kickstarter in late 2001 or early 2002. He and I met in New York in 2005 and quickly became friends. Soon Perry told me about his idea: a website where people could ask the public for financial support for ideas. Like patronage, except the money would come from people on the internet rather than sixteenth-century popes and rich uncles. And with a twist: if projects didn't reach their funding goal by a deadline, no money would change hands.

I remember not liking the idea at first. I told Perry it reminded me of *American Idol*. But after talking about it more, I was in. Perry was CEO, I was cofounder and head of our community, and Charles Adler joined as cofounder and head of design not long after. The three of us and a lot of other people worked very hard to make Kickstarter and put it into the world.

At the moment I write this, billions of dollars have been put into the hands of creative people through Kickstarter since it launched in 2009. More than 100,000 new ideas exist because of it. Public art by Ai Weiwei, Oscar-winning movies, Grammy-winning albums, new fields of technology, and thousands of books, artworks, and other creative projects are just some of the things created through Kickstarter.

Kickstarter is a globally recognized tool, but little about it has ever been typical. From the beginning we exclusively focused on helping creative projects come to life. We didn't want to be everything to everybody. The goal was to make something that mattered, and to do it for the long haul. We said publicly that we'd never sell the company or take it public. We would do what was best for Kickstarter's mission, not use it to do what was best for us.

Unlike Silicon Valley companies burning through piles of cash, we stayed small and lived within our means. Kickstarter began operating profitably in its fourteenth month in business. A bit more than one hundred people work out of Kickstarter's office, an old pencil factory in Brooklyn that the company bought years ago. Kickstarter doesn't even have a landlord.

It was this same independent spirit that led Kickstarter to

become a public benefit corporation (PBC). A PBC is a for-profit company that's legally committed to balancing shareholder interests with producing a positive benefit for society. In 2015 Kickstarter became a PBC, explicitly setting higher standards for its conduct and impact. Kickstarter and Patagonia are two of the best-known companies to have made this conversion.

Kickstarter also inspired the broader industry of crowdfunding. Though we weren't the first to launch such a site, the look, feel, and functionality of crowdfunding is based on Kickstarter. A lot of online political fund-raising, too. (Sorry about that.)

Crowdfunding is one of those ideas that seems obvious now. Groups of people putting small amounts of money together to create collective action. It seems as natural as air.

It wasn't. The idea of people giving each other money just because they were asked seems totally normal now. But it seemed very strange when we started telling people about it more than a decade ago.

I remember meetings with potential investors, creators, and others who we hoped would connect with the idea. Many people did. Others rejected it outright.

"Nobody's going to give a stranger money," they would say. "The world doesn't work that way."

These people would tell us to make Kickstarter more like an investment: "Give me financial upside in projects. That's how the real world works."

That's exactly the world I wanted to change. I wanted to break free of the universe where an idea had to justify its existence based on how much money it would make somebody else. How limiting!

This disregard for "how the real world works" let us think a step beyond how things were. It gave us a wider spectrum of what could be possible.

Ten years later, billions of dollars have changed hands and tens of millions of people have experienced crowdfunding just the way it was imagined. Through Kickstarter, GoFundMe, and others. A whole new economy based on the generosity of people supporting a fellow human being or idea.

The status quo's view of what's possible was too limited. It often is.

■ ■ ■ ■

Crowdfunding is far from the only human-made thing we think of as natural.

What a piano looks like, why we drink orange juice for breakfast, the shape of the letters you read right now. We can't imagine the world without these things. We think of them as "how it is." But those are all concepts that were totally made up by someone just like you or me.

I was brought up believing in an orderly world where things make sense. There's no need to worry. History is logical. People in charge know what's going on. Everything will be fine.

There's some version of this that we all still believe. But it's not true.

The truth is that everything is made up. The same way

Kickstarter was made up. Some people think of something and try to bring it into existence. If other people start believing in this new idea, it becomes real.

Did you know that the high five was invented in 1977 during the middle of a baseball game?

"It was a wild, triumphant moment . . . [Glenn] Burke, waiting on deck, thrust his hand enthusiastically over his head to greet his friend at the plate. [Dusty] Baker, not knowing what to do, smacked it. 'His hand was up in the air, and he was arching way back,' says Baker. . . . 'So I reached up and hit his hand. It seemed like the thing to do.'"

You hear that phrase a lot when it comes to new ideas: "it seemed like the thing to do." If other people agree—as people did with the high five—it becomes A Thing. There's no steering committee that gives the green light. There's no stamp of approval. There's not a grand design. It just happens.

The truth is there is little order. The status quo persists because people continue to wake up and believe in these ideas each day. Or they're so deeply embedded we don't recognize them as ideas anymore.

This is both obvious and hard to wrap our minds around. Or at least it was for me. I objectively knew this but didn't truly understand it for most of my life.

Then Kickstarter happened. Me, an ordinary person from a farm in rural Virginia, made a ripple in the world. It showed me that things were way more fragile than I was taught to believe.

Once I started seeing the world this way, I couldn't unsee it.

．．．．

In 2015 I was invited to give a speech at a big tech conference in Dublin, Ireland, called Web Summit. Tens of thousands of people would be there. I wanted to make it count.

In this talk I shared the first seeds of this idea. That a small segment of our society was using our movies, our music, our neighborhoods, our everything, as an investment portfolio. Our world had been overtaken by an insatiable need for money to make more money.

It was a twenty-minute pitch to a room of thousands of tech people to rethink how we're operating. We can't accept the inevitability of what's happening. We have to find a way out. I proposed we turn our backs on these forces and create a new path. I used Kickstarter as an example of a way it could be done. We had maintained our idealism and independence by not financially maximizing. If companies were willing to make different choices, they could, too.

Normally I would be onstage selling people on using Kickstarter. What was I selling instead—*not* selling? Who wants to buy that? These aren't the kinds of things you're supposed to say.

I was more nervous than I've ever been giving a speech. But stronger than my fears was a conviction that these ideas would matter more if I, then the CEO of a name-brand company, used my airtime to say this. What made it scary to me was the very thing that could make it meaningful to others.

Afterward, I met people from the audience who were moved

to hear someone articulate these ideas. That encouraged me to share them more. In talks with audiences in Barcelona, Berlin, London, Mexico City, Norway, Seoul, Tokyo, New York, Orlando, Chicago, and Jackson, Mississippi. In every one of those rooms I discovered a similar yearning for a new way to think about the future.

. . . .

Kickstarter gave me a unique window into how ideas work. Both through the experience of cofounding the platform, and by watching thousands of ideas come to life through it.

When we first started telling people about Kickstarter, there was no website to point people to. The term "crowdfunding" was years away from being known. Using only words, we had to describe the idea in a way that people would understand and get excited by.

This wasn't easy to do. Remember that even I didn't like the idea the first time I heard it. But the more you talk about something, the more you learn what works about it and what doesn't. Through practice and iteration, we learned to talk about Kickstarter in a way that people connected with.

Eventually I could even tell when someone had stopped listening to me. "Oh no, I've lost them," I'd think, as I watched their eyes glaze over while I tried to explain the idea. I'd make a note to find a better way to say whatever I'd just been saying in the future and shift topics to regain their attention.

Sometimes these conversations were with skeptics, like the potential investors who wanted financial upside in projects. But there were many early believers, too. Our creative friends especially got it. They lived the problem Kickstarter was created to solve. They knew firsthand how limited the paths to funding were. It's no coincidence that some of Kickstarter's earliest investors came from the creative world.

The day after Kickstarter launched in 2009, I wrote a blog post titled "Why Kickstarter?" It reads:

> The Beatles were turned down by nearly every record label. George Lucas couldn't find a movie studio that would make *Star Wars*. Bob Woodward and Carl Bernstein of the *Washington Post* were two of the only reporters assigned to cover Watergate. John Kennedy Toole went to his grave with *A Confederacy of Dunces* still unpublished.
>
> Anecdotes like these have become folklore, as have their lessons: good ideas go unrecognized, experts get it wrong, perseverance prevails. All true. [But] it's also worth considering that maybe this judgment system that seems to get so much so wrong is outdated. That it doesn't speak for anyone except itself. That a good idea, well-crafted and pursued with passion, doesn't need a gatekeeper's stamp of approval to succeed.
>
> The gauntlet that is fund-raising (for everyone who doesn't have a rich, benevolent uncle) sees only profit or predictability. Not art or passion or talent or an incredible story of inspiration.
>
> Kickstarter aims to give each one of us a chance to fund our ideas, starting directly with the people who are closest to

it (friends, fans, community-fellows). And it's a way to break beyond the traditional methods—loans, investment, industry deals, grants—to discover that we can offer each other value through creation without a middleman dictating the product and terms.

I had no idea whether Kickstarter would ever get close to these lofty goals when I wrote this. A decade later it has and then some. Kickstarter and others established a new possibility for funding creative projects and ideas that's now accepted and mainstream.

Many Kickstarter projects underwent a similar transition from new and unproven idea to mainstream acceptance.

The tabletop game Cards Against Humanity started as a Kickstarter project backed by several hundred people. So did Oculus Rift, which was a prototype in a garage when its Kickstarter launched. Pebble invented smartwatches with its string of Kickstarter projects. Hundreds of restaurants, movie theaters, galleries, and other public spaces are open today thanks to their backers and the platform. All these projects began as ideas just like Kickstarter itself.

During Kickstarter's first year, I reviewed nearly every project when it launched. Over the years I personally helped musicians, artists, dancers, game makers, technologists, designers, filmmakers, and others put almost every kind of creative project you can imagine into the world. I even advised masters like Neil Young and Spike Lee and got a close glimpse at how they work.

In 2011, I began working with award-winning documentarian Jehane Noujaim on a project to fund a film called *The Square*. It was during the Arab Spring protests, and she and her crew were filming in Cairo's Tahrir Square. The filmmakers were following several of the leaders of the uprising as it was happening. One day Jehane sent a clip from a recent day's filming, which included the cameraperson being pinned down by government gunfire behind a doorway, the camera heaving as the cinematographer caught their breath. The film was nominated for Best Documentary at the Oscars three years later.

I've been around enough good and bad ideas to know when something works and when it doesn't. And as I've talked about financial maximization with people around the world, it's felt like talking to creators about the challenge of funding ideas in the days before Kickstarter. Awareness of the problem is acute and widespread.

I felt it when, early on, I pitched the book to classmates in a leadership program and a peer from Myanmar took out his wallet and handed me $20, saying he wanted to buy the first copy. I felt it when a preacher in Mississippi offered encouragement after hearing early ideas. I felt it in Abu Dhabi when a Muslim man thanked me for defending the importance of nonfinancial values.

Execution is a critical gap between idea and reality, but it's not the only one. Another is belief. For ideas to matter, people have to believe in them. There's only so much an idea can do on its own. Ideas need supporters, carriers, and executors to become real.

The fact that more of us are coming to recognize the limits of financial maximization matters. That's a meaningful step toward change. Even if you're not in a position of authority, this is true.

In the past, the only people that mattered were the popes, kings, boards of directors, and executives in corner offices. But today, all of our voices matter. We all have the power to influence the world. It's just a matter of learning how to do it.

■ ■ ■ ■

Maybe this idea of financial maximization sounds interesting in theory to you. A good dinner-party conversation. But I believe it's more than that. Major changes are coming whether we're ready or not.

A massively growing population (about 10 billion people by 2050, almost double what it was in 2000), increasing inequality, environmental pressures, and technological shifts are changing the world. The mix of population growth and resource constraints alone creates challenging equations without clear answers.

And yet even as the seas rise and species die, we continue to prioritize financial maximization. We struggle to see how any other way of operating is possible.

We watch this car crash thinking we're outside it. Other People are the cause of it and Other People will fix it and Other People will suffer the consequences if they don't. Every single one of us has it in our minds that we're separate from it all.

Instead we blame others and pray for a Superman-like solution. That some genius figures out how to purify the air and the oceans and Warren Buffett and Oprah agree to pay for it. Or, even better, we learn that Steve Jobs's previously unknown last product was a device that solves everything by giving every user total cosmic clarity. His last words, "Oh wow. Oh wow. Oh wow," were also the first words of iUs, his final user experience.

But hope isn't a plan. When a Hail Mary is the strategy, you've already lost. And yet on the big questions in front of us, we act as if there's nothing worth working toward.

The moral philosopher Will MacAskill once shared an insight about how old humankind actually is: if you compare *Homo sapiens* to other species on Earth, humans are the equivalent of ten years old in our species' life span. Not even adolescent. Meaning that there should be many tens of thousands of years of human history ahead of us. And yet we act like this is the last party. Who cares whether anybody cleans anything up?

What a crazy place for humankind—so hopeful about the future so recently—to be. It's madness.

I don't believe the world is doomed or that hope is lost.

The world changes for the better all the time. But noticing isn't easy. Watching for change is like watching grass grow. Invisible in the now but always there.

When society undergoes major change, people discover that the world isn't as solid as they thought. I learned that in my humble way with Kickstarter. It changed me. I felt like I gained sight. I could better see the world for what it was.

In the pages ahead, I hope to create that same feeling in you.

CHAPTER TWO

THE NO-LEFT-TURN RULE

PICTURE YOUR COMMUTE TO WORK.

You get into your car. You back out of your driveway. You turn off your street, get onto the bypass, and drive twenty minutes. Five minutes later you pull into a parking spot.

Now think back. What stores did you see on the right-hand side of the road on your way there?

Americans who commute from a residential area to a commercial area are likely to see gas stations, Starbucks, Dunkin' Donuts, and other breakfast drive-throughs on the right-hand side of the road. The kinds of things people tend to want in the morning.

Now picture the drive home. What do you see on the right-hand side then?

When those same Americans commute home to a residential

area, they're likely to see shopping centers, grocery stores, and restaurants on the right-hand side of the road. Things people tend to want *after* work.

The placement of businesses with or against traffic comes from something called the "no-left-turn rule" in the world of retail planning.

In retail, few things are as important as drop-in customers. And one of the biggest factors in attracting drop-ins is which side of the street you're on.

The goal is to be a right turn at the right time of day. Before-work businesses like coffee shops should be on the right-hand side of morning traffic. After-work businesses like grocery stores should be on the right-hand side of evening traffic.

People are that much more likely to turn right than left. It can take minutes to turn against traffic. Not many people have the patience. Turning right is faster, safer, and, thanks to optimizations by retail planners, the way traffic overwhelmingly flows.

Ever gotten off the highway to get gas only to find that all the gas stations are on the other side of the road?

This is the no-left-turn rule in action. You're driving against the expected flow of traffic.

Q: Why did the customer cross the road?

A: They didn't.

HIDDEN DEFAULTS

The no-left-turn rule is an example of a hidden default. An unseen influence on our behavior. Hidden defaults are subtle nudges that guide us, like the white lines of a parking lot, as Harvard Law School professor Cass Sunstein has written. The modern world is full of these hidden defaults. And for good reason: they're very effective.

Take organ donation rates. You would expect a country's cultural beliefs around death to determine whether people choose to donate their organs or not. In reality we exercise less choice than we think.

Here are the percentages of people who chose to donate their organs in different European countries:

Organ donation rates

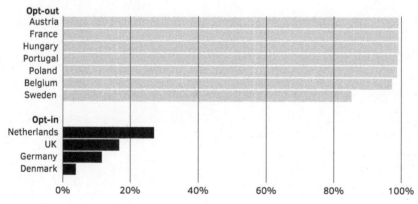

SOURCE: JOHNSON AND GOLDSTEIN 2003

Notice the huge differences between countries that seem similar, like Austria and Germany. Do Austrians and Germans have beliefs around death that are so different from one another?

No. They just have different forms to fill out. In Austria, citizens are default opted-in to have their organs donated. In Germany, citizens are default opted-out.

We tend to go along with the default in front of us. Whatever it happens to be.

Sixty-seven percent of people with gym memberships don't use them but keep paying anyway. Just 0.28 percent of email addresses opt out of marketing newsletters; 99.7 percent passively choose to keep getting spammed.

Here are reelection rates for the US House of Representatives over the past fifty years:

US House of Representatives reelection rate

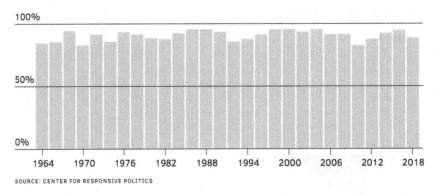

SOURCE: CENTER FOR RESPONSIVE POLITICS

You may be thinking, but sitting congresspeople enjoy all sorts of structural advantages. It's easier for them to raise money.

The job allows them to do favors. They're more well-known. How is that a hidden default?

And that's exactly it. Hidden defaults don't just happen. They accrue. They grow. They develop. By people using knowledge and power to change the defaults in their favor over time.

This happens for legitimate reasons (left turns are more dangerous than right ones; extra healthy human organs are useful for people with unhealthy ones) and less legitimate reasons, as we'll see.

Here's that same congressional reelection rate, now with Congress's public approval rate layered on top. Notice a pattern?

Even as our dissatisfaction goes up, our reliance on the default at the root of it does, too. It defaults us into submission.

US House of Representatives reelection rate vs. approval rate

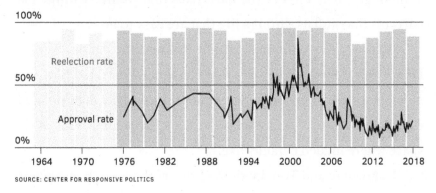

SOURCE: CENTER FOR RESPONSIVE POLITICS

This is how primed we are to follow defaults. We're grateful for them even when we don't like them. One less thing to worry about.

THE HIDDEN DEFAULT OF FINANCIAL MAXIMIZATION

Some defaults we can see and change. You can go paperless with your credit card bill. You can adjust your notifications settings. Others we can hardly see at all.

A David Foster Wallace story illustrates this well.

An old fish and a young fish are swimming in the ocean.

The old fish says, "How's the water today?"

The young fish replies, "What's water?"

It isn't easy to see the world in context. If only it were as concrete as Jim Carrey touching the wall in *The Truman Show*. But it isn't.

Hidden defaults are deeply a part of us. They're the customs, traditions, and social codes that form our tribes and nations. The rituals around births, weddings, and death. Why we wear one color and not another. They're the narratives that we live within. The currents that pull us through life that are easy to miss.

Behavioral economists Daniel Kahneman, Amos Tversky, Dan Ariely, Iris Bohnet, and others have demonstrated how susceptible we are to influence. Our choices are easily manipulated, especially when we're not conscious it's happening. This is the space where hidden defaults live.

Kahneman and Tversky showed this with research on anchoring and bias—how the presence of a single word or irrelevant but memorable piece of information will shift our behavior. Ariely demonstrated how our emotions affect our choices and words like "free" change how we think. We believe our actions are based on objective truth. They're often guided by hidden defaults instead.

This book is concerned with one hidden default in particular. An unseen force that I believe has as much influence on the world as any other. A magnetic north that tugs us in its direction.

That's the hidden default of financial maximization. Financial maximization says that in any decision, the rational choice is the one that makes the most money. This is the underlying "why" behind many of our choices. The right-hand turn of modern life.

Financial maximization defines our idea of rational progress. Arguably our core metric of progress over the past century has been gross domestic product, which largely measures how good we are at financial maximization. However GDP makes no assessment of the money's larger implications, only how much of it there is.

Once you realize how we're measuring success, everything falls into place.

It's how America justifies a health care system that causes 62 percent of personal bankruptcies. Health care providers, drugmakers, and insurance companies increase profits through a Byzantine and pocket-emptying system built to financially maximize.

It's why the prices of already existing, critical drugs keep rising for patients while the pharmaceutical companies making those drugs reap growing profits.

It's also why companies used more of their profits on stock buybacks in 2018 than they spent on R&D or raising pay. Shareholders and the stock price are the priority, not workers or the future.

As they say in product development, you are what you measure.

· · · ·

While we expect the world of finance to operate according to the goal of financial maximization, the dogma now dominates fields beyond business as well.

Education, government, health care, and science are increasingly driven by the philosophies of financial maximization. Institutions that had previously been focused on a range of outcomes—knowledge, service, care, discovery—are increasingly measured by just one: money.

Imagine it this way.

Each of these fields—education, government, health care, and science—is a large stone building. Some hulking thing you'd see in Paris or Manhattan.

It took centuries to lay the groundwork for these buildings. Their first foundations were put down in Genesis, in the hieroglyphs of Mesopotamia and Egypt, in Plato's *Republic*, in Newton's laws, and so on.

The buildings went up painstakingly at first. Every brick was a major achievement. But as knowledge spread, construction timelines sped from centuries to decades.

Each building contains all facets of this effort. The philosophies and ideas that first sparked its existence. The traditions and rituals that hold its culture and values. The generations of women and men who distribute its benefits and knowledge. The young who dream of joining their ranks. During the twentieth century, America pointed to its buildings as evidence of its greatness. See what wonders a democratic society can produce? The world was impressed.

That's not to say things are perfect.

The buildings are often the subject of debate. Politicians argue over their construction, their contents, and their membership. What should be included? What should not? Who should be allowed to join? In what capacity?

Tensions between those who believe the buildings are finished and those who want to add to them are frequent. The emergence of new knowledge or a new building will inevitably threaten some part of the existing order. The debates can spark cultural divides, like whether to teach evolution in schools or the morality of stem cell research.

To date, the buildings have weathered these storms and evolved with the times. But as the twentieth century neared its end, the spirit changed, too. A new energy took its place.

When the dominant perspective of today looks at the buildings, it recognizes the importance of education, government, health care, and science. It sees their value to society. And then it analyzes the upside.

Huge target market. Mega profit potential. How much for it?

Today's perspective doesn't see institutions. It sees assets. It sees money. Like bank robbers divvying up a score.

Any discussion of the purpose of the buildings, what renovations they're in need of, or the people who depend on them is less important than who gets to own what.

Their output gets the same treatment. Social services like education and health care that were once nominal in cost now come at a significant price. As the buildings have been carved up and sold off, the public has been forced to pay the bill.

This is what it means to be dominated by a default of financial maximization. It means viewing our society as a portfolio to buy, sell, and trade. It's like seeing the world through the eyes of a sociopathic oligarch. Everything has a price.

A RATIONAL ORIGIN

It all started innocently enough.

In 1776, the Scottish economist and philosopher Adam Smith argued that society best functions when people are trusted to act according to their self-interest. "It is not from the benevolence of the butcher, the brewer, or the baker that we expect our dinner, but from their regard to their own interest," he famously wrote in *The Wealth of Nations.*

You didn't have to force or beg a butcher to be a butcher. Because this was what enabled people to survive and meet the needs of their family, it's what they would do on their own. This was an empowering idea. A society built on trusting people to look out for themselves was possible—and preferable.

Smith believed that the "invisible hand" of our collective

individual wills would maintain a balance of power between capital, land, and workers. This balance would create a continuous cycle of production, reinvestment, and improvement that would benefit everyone.

Quite a lovely idea, don't you think?

But note that Smith didn't say that the butcher must maximize hog slaughter rates, lower standards to an acceptable minimum, and underpay and overwork laborers to maximize those profits, and then redirect that money to executives and investors instead.

For many companies today, however, strategies like these are standard. It's what investors expect companies to do. It's what many people think capitalism *is*. If companies don't do everything they can to financially maximize, investors may bring in new leaders who will.

Adam Smith believed strongly in the importance of profits. They were how companies would raise wages and invest in better, more specialized goods and services, and how society would ultimately grow. But they weren't just an end in themselves.

The financial maximization that dominates the world today is something different. And it appeared more recently than we think.

■ ■ ■

In the early 1950s, the United States emerged from the Second World War as a new global force. The decade before, America dropped the first (and hopefully only) atomic bombs in history, on Japan. They unleashed unprecedented power that became even scarier after the Soviet Union got the bomb, too. As the two nations faced off, the newly invented Doomsday Clock—created to reflect mankind's proximity to self-annihilation—read just two minutes from the apocalypse.

The Defense Department asked a group of scientists and mathematicians at an elite think tank called the RAND Corporation to come up with a strategy for what the United States should do in this new nuclear age.

To study the situation, the researchers turned to a then-new field called game theory. Game theory uses mathematical models to determine the optimal, rational strategies in games and other strategic conflicts.

When applied to the nuclear standoff with the Soviet Union, game theory allowed the scientists to consider different approaches the United States might take, how the USSR might respond, and where things might go from there. This greatly expanded the decision makers' awareness of the potential outcomes of whatever strategy they considered.

The RAND scientists created a variety of scenarios to explore different kinds of conflicts. Many of these scenarios were interactive games that people would play. Arguably the most famous example of a game theory scenario, called Prisoner's Dilemma, was created at RAND in 1950. It goes like this.

You and a partner have robbed a bank. You're both arrested and put in separate interrogation rooms. The police offer each of you the same deal:

If you rat out your partner and your partner stays silent, you'll go free and your partner will go to jail for three years.

If your partner rats you out and you stay silent, you'll go to jail for three years and your partner will go free.

If you both rat each other out, both of you will go to jail for two years.

If neither of you talk, both of you will go to jail for one year.

Since you're both in interrogation booths and neither knows what the other will do, it's impossible to determine the "right" answer. Instead you must act in part based on how you think your partner will act.

Prisoner's Dilemma illustrates the unexpected outcomes of game theory's notion of rationality. In *The Compleat Strategyst*, a book published by RAND about game theory in 1954, the author writes that game theory "takes the position that there is a definite way that rational people should behave."

It goes on:

> The notion that there is some way people ought to behave does not refer to an obligation based on law or ethics. Rather it refers to a kind of mathematical morality, or at least frugality, which claims that the *sensible object of the player is to gain as much from the game as he can, safely, in the face of a skillful opponent who is pursuing an antithetical goal.* This is our model of rational behavior.

According to this model of rational behavior, what's the optimal strategy in Prisoner's Dilemma? To rat out your partner. In part, because it's the only way you can go free.

You put yourself at greater risk by trusting your partner. It's less risky to look out only for yourself. And if you can see that, surely your so-called partner in the other interrogation room can see it, too. The cycle of paranoia goes on from there.

Values like honor and loyalty encourage us to stick together with our partner against the authorities. But according to this new, rational way of looking at the world, this was incorrect. Sticking together was too risky. The rational thing was to rat your partner out first.

But note what happens when neither player talks: less time is served overall—a total of two years between two people, versus three years for one person. It's the best overall outcome, but it's only possible if neither player pursues a strategy of maximizing his or her immediate self-interest.

Some of the first people to play Prisoner's Dilemma were the secretaries at RAND. Many of them chose to stay loyal to their partners. Their relationships were what mattered to them. The secretaries achieved the ideal outcome of the game.

According to the model of rationality set by game theory, the secretaries weren't playing correctly. Pursuing your immediate self-interest was the rational thing to do.

■ ■ ■ ■

The RAND Corporation published *The Compleat Strategyst* with the goal of expanding the application of game theory in day-to-day life. "We believe it possible that Game Theory, as it develops—or something like it—may become an important concept and force in many phases of life," author J. D. Williams wrote.

They were right. Game theory became a tool for a new kind of "hyperrational" way of thinking. A view that, among other things, teaches the rationality of maximizing one's self-interest.

This way of thinking brought benefits just as the RAND scientists thought. But it also came with side effects. Most notably a more individualistic—and even paranoid—way of looking at the world.

In the opening pages of *The Compleat Strategyst*, the author asks us to imagine we're sitting at a game of poker with four other people. But, the author suddenly adds, two of the players may have "formed a coalition, in advance of the game, in which they agreed to pool their winnings or losses." Even in the already adversarial game of poker, the game theory perspective raises the stakes further. People are conspiring to cheat you. The game is a trap. What are you going to do about it?

This was a dark step from Adam Smith's notion of self-interest. For Smith, self-interest was a vehicle for trust. You could trust the butcher to do what was best for the butcher. Now that same idea was used to justify the rationality of distrust. How much could you actually trust the butcher? What goes on in there anyway? You're foolish to trust anyone but yourself.

This mind-set guided the United States' strategy toward the Soviet Union in the Cold War. Which, considering the stakes, was probably wise. But it wasn't long before the philosophy spread into everyday life, just as the game theorists predicted. We were each in our own miniature cold wars. Everyone trying to get theirs. Everyone against everyone else. This was the cold, hard reality of life. There was math to prove it.

THE GAMES WE PLAY

Despite its rationality, Prisoner's Dilemma has a blind spot. It has its own hidden default that strongly shapes its moral of the superiority of self-interest.

It's the interrogation rooms—not some grand cosmic truth— that are most responsible for the moral of the game. They are what keep the player isolated from the world. Not the world itself.

If you were to imagine the same scenario outside an interrogation room—say, a Clue-like dinner party—the notion of a zero-sum fight to the death between Colonel Mustard and Mrs. Peacock seems absurd. It's far easier to imagine collaborating to confuse the authorities and living to see another day.

And it's true. Within game theory, Prisoner's Dilemma is classified as a noncooperative game, meaning the scenario is hostile by design. It's just as rational to approach such a situation cooperatively, as another famous game theory scenario called Stag Hunt shows.

This game works similarly to Prisoner's Dilemma. The player has two choices:

Hunt on your own and get a small reward.

Hunt with the other player and get a bigger reward.

But if one player chooses to hunt together and the other

chooses to hunt alone, the person who chose to hunt together gets nothing.

The players aren't allowed to consult each other before choosing, so you're just as likely to end up losing by trusting your partner as you are in Prisoner's Dilemma. But the game structure clearly demonstrates that by collaborating you will enjoy the greatest success.

Prisoner's Dilemma and Stag Hunt are two rational but fundamentally different ways of looking at the world. One is competitive: Earth is a planet of people plotting in interrogation rooms against one another. The other is cooperative: if we hunt together we'll get more food.

In both games cooperation brings the greatest reward. But in only one does the game reveal the truth to the players.

. . . .

A fascinating study illustrates just how important these cues about how to play really are.

Researchers set up two different Prisoner's Dilemma games for subjects to play. The rules of both games were similar to the scenario described earlier.

The only difference between the two games was their name. One was called the Wall Street Game. The other was called the Community Game. The researchers ran the two games with Stanford students and Israeli air force pilots. The results were similar for both.

People playing the Wall Street Game were more likely to turn on their partners to get a bigger individual reward than those playing the Community Game. Wall Street Game players expected their counterparts to turn on them, so they turned on them first. It was the rational thing to do.

When playing the scenario called the Community Game, the results were very different. The same players that were disloyal in the Wall Street Game instead stuck together. Considering it was called the Community Game, this was also the rational thing to do.

When playing the Wall Street version, less than 40 percent of players chose to stay loyal. When playing the Community Game version, nearly 70 percent of them did. The same game, just different names.

Is it a Wall Street world or a Community world? A Prisoner's Dilemma world or a Stag Hunt world? Part of it comes down to just what we call it. That's how powerful hidden defaults can be.

HIDDEN DEFAULTS SET WHAT'S NORMAL

By setting the context, hidden defaults make decisions for us. We refer to this context obliquely as "how things are done" or "how it is." It's "what's normal." These phrases identify places where the individual isn't making the decision; rather, the choice has already been made for us by someone or something else.

These hidden defaults even determine what we perceive as fact. We think we make decisions based on objective truth, but all of us follow norms and defaults set by the cultural narratives we live within. Just like in the Community and Wall Street games.

This leads to the final and most challenging thing about hidden defaults.

Not only do we perceive hidden defaults as how things are, we see them as how they *should* be.

How things are is how they should be, we often think. Because of this, we find it very difficult to imagine the world being any other way.

The sociologist Max Weber wrote about how an iron cage of rationality can trap us. Eventually we come to think the cage itself is a product of the natural world. Sure, it's a cage, but it's *supposed* to be here!

But if we look backward, we can clearly see that the world that existed before was very different. Somehow we got to here from there. And we'll get from here to somewhere else. The cage is never as solid as we think.

CHAPTER THREE

WHY EVERYTHING
IS THE SAME

IN 2017, A SONG BY A COUNTRY SINGER NAMED SAM HUNT did something no song had done before.

For eight straight months—thirty-four consecutive weeks—Hunt's ballad "Body Like a Back Road" topped the *Billboard* Hot Country Songs chart. It was the longest reign at the top of a *Billboard* chart in music history. Longer than any song by Elvis, the Beatles, Frank Sinatra, Michael Jackson, or Madonna. Longer than any song ever.

"Body Like a Back Road" as the most enduring #1 of all time seems like a crazy outlier. A glitch in the matrix. But it's not. It's the logical conclusion of a trend.

Turn on the radio and you hear it. Go to the movies and you see it. Walk through a city or small town and you feel it. Once financial maximization took over, everything started becoming the same.

THE SONG STAYS THE SAME

Radio isn't what it used to be, but it remains powerful. It's still a top destination for discovering new music. It's where the emergency alert system sends instructions in the event of a disaster. The majority of Americans listen to it every day.

We've witnessed the decline of radio, so we see it as an outdated technology. But radio's appearance in the 1920s was as earthshaking as the internet's in the 1990s.

Many of the sentiments that celebrated the launch of the internet were first used to herald radio. With radio, anyone could broadcast on an open spectrum created by Mother Nature and made accessible by science. It was revolutionary and democratic.

Radio was the first truly mass communications channel. The first way humans could instantly communicate across continents and oceans with their voices. The power of God in the hands of man.

The people ushering in radio were aware of its implications. Not long after the radio spectrum debuted, Congress set an ownership limit of two stations per entity. Officials said this was needed to keep this new resource from concentrating in too few hands. Radio was a public trust. Under this mind-set, radio flourished. Every community had its own station, its own voice.

But it wasn't long before a counterargument appeared.

Disarmingly, it took the same angle used to justify setting limits on ownership. About the importance of every voice being heard. And then it argued that these limits discriminated against companies and their owners. What if these entities wanted to own ten stations? Or a hundred? Don't they have rights, too?

In 1943, radio networks sued the government, alleging that the rules violated their First Amendment rights by restraining their speech. Courts upheld the regulations, but the seeds of a coming revolution were planted.

Under intense political and legal pressure, the rules meant to protect radio were steadily weakened based on an argument that not having any rules would be more democratic and more fair.

The change started gradually. Just lifting the cap from two stations to five. Then from five to seven. But each time the cap got raised, the next expansion became a foregone conclusion. Bigger companies could buy more influence.

By 1982, the head of the agency responsible for overseeing radio announced he was deferring to station owners pretty much completely. "Commercial broadcasting is a business . . . not fiduciaries of the public," he stated. The government would now, "so far as possible, defer to a broadcaster's judgment." The argument was that an open marketplace where stations were competing for profits would make for better and more diverse radio than one where stations were held to a defined public interest.

In 1984, the ownership cap went from seven stations to forty. And in 1996 to virtually no limits at all. Within a year, 4,000 of the 11,000 radio stations in America were bought. By 2002, the largest radio station owner, Clear Channel Communications, controlled more than 1,200 radio stations in America. More than thirty times the legal limit of just ten years before.

Today, half of all radio stations in America are owned by just two companies. The same resource that officials thought so important that no one could own more than two of them is now dominated by just two companies. Period.

Once radio was under conglomerate control, layoffs started. Me included. My first writing job in New York was with a small company that Clear Channel acquired about a year after I joined. Two years later, Clear Channel laid me off. I wasn't alone. Even DJs got the ax then, too.

Why pay for local DJs and programmers when you can have someone at HQ press play on a thousand stations at once? Stations with the same owners began sharing as much as a 97 percent overlap in the songs they played. Costs went down. Profits went up. And playlists stopped changing.

The number of different songs to top the charts each year began to fall. From a new #1 nearly every week in the 1980s to the monotony of today.

Number of different country songs that hit #1 on the Billboard Hot Country chart, by year

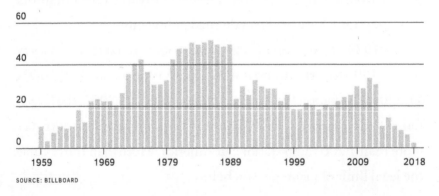

SOURCE: BILLBOARD

This is part of how "Body Like a Back Road" came to be the biggest hit of all time. Thousands of stations playing the same playlists day and night. An orchestra of maximizing efficiency.

SEQUEL TO A SEQUEL

It's not just the airwaves that are increasingly monotonous. The movies are, too.

Of the ten most popular films at the box office in each of the years 2013, 2014, and 2015, only one was based on an original idea. The other twenty-nine were sequels, prequels, or adaptations of stories that already existed. In both 2017 and 2018, *all ten* of the highest-grossing movies were sequels or adaptations of existing material.

Here are the number of prequels, sequels, remakes, and reboots in the box office top ten each year since 1950.

Number of prequels, sequels, remakes, and reboots in box office top ten

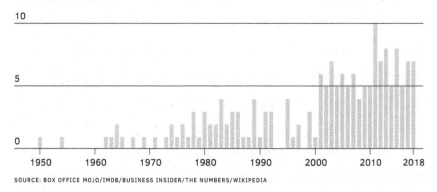

SOURCE: BOX OFFICE MOJO/IMDB/BUSINESS INSIDER/THE NUMBERS/WIKIPEDIA

The left side of the graph is when Hollywood was telling new stories. The right side is when Hollywood figured out how much easier it was to retell a story that someone else had already told. In the last fifteen years, 61 percent of Hollywood movies have been remakes, sequels, or adaptations.

This shift in strategy coincided with a shift in ownership. In the 1980s, owning a Hollywood studio became the rage in corporate fashion. Oil companies, Japanese electronics companies, an Australian newspaper publisher, a Canadian booze conglomerate, and even Coca-Cola bought significant stakes in movie studios.

The multinational conglomerates weren't making these acquisitions out of a newfound love of film. They bought them to make money. After the dawn of the blockbuster era in the 1970s, big corporate checks came rolling in. The decision makers changed and the movies did, too.

According to their business models, sequels produced better financial returns. Making remakes and sequels is "tried and true and lessens the risk," an industry expert told ABC. "It's why movie sequels really began."

Movies started to feel like any other product these companies sold. There was the Diet version, the Extreme version, the Woman version (sometimes), the Elderly version (sometimes), the African American version (less often), and so on. Going to the movies started feeling like going to the cereal aisle. A million choices, all kind of the same.

The culture around film changed as well. *Variety* began reporting weekly box office returns for the first time in the 1980s.

Movies started being judged on their opening weekend numbers even more than the reviews. With so much at stake and movies costing more than ever, studios became more conservative and the diversity of ideas decreased.

Saying movies have gone downhill is hardly controversial. But what about TV? The kinds of shows Netflix, HBO, AMC, and others make are original and diverse. Doesn't that disprove this point?

Traditional broadcast television, which follows a similar business logic as movies, absolutely suffers from these same forces. Sitcoms, cop, doctor, and lawyer shows are rarely known for their originality.

But it's also true that prestige television operates on a level above movies and broadcast TV. It's where some of the most original and forward-thinking creative work happens.

Virtually all of these shows are made by newer players wanting to establish credibility. When they make prestige TV they're not financially maximizing, they're reputationally maximizing. Their goal is to impress. ("It's not TV. It's HBO.")

Consider how we judge prestige TV compared to movies. There's no equivalent of a box office for these kinds of shows. Not even viewership numbers are consistently shared. Their success or failure is almost entirely determined by the response of critics and viewers. The viewer and producer are aligned around a shared goal. Financial concerns are, within reason, secondary to the quality of the work and its impact on the platform's reputation. That's why critics will call an unwatched prestige TV show slept on, and an unwatched Hollywood movie a flop. Their intentions are different.

We can't assume prestige TV's current dynamic will last forever, however. Many markets start out this way, with many players creating a diverse ecosystem. But as a few players tighten control, the dynamics change. The need for prestige lessens and the demand for profits grows. It's not long before the new world starts looking a lot like the old one.

If financial maximization was merely making the radio boring and turning every movie into a sequel now in IMAX and 3-D, it would be almost funny. But these forces are changing more than just music and movies. They're even changing our neighborhoods.

GENTRIFICATION

At the corner of Second Avenue and First Street in the Lower East Side of New York City stands a TD Bank. An advertisement hangs in the window: "My perfect Saturday would be banking on Sunday."

Inside are rows of cubicles where bankers can meet customers. But not many people come into this location. They don't have to. Four other TD Banks are within a fifteen-minute walk from here.

That's if you bank with TD. If you include other banks, there are more than two dozen branches nearby.

In recent decades, the number of bank branches in Manhattan has grown considerably. In 2014 there were 1,763 banks in New York City. That's 461 more than a decade before. It's as if the ATM were never invented.

■ ■ ■ ■

It's 1985. We're standing at the same corner: Second Avenue and First Street. On the same spot where TD Bank stands in 2019, a dive bar called Mars Bar stands today.

Mars Bar was opened by a man from Queens named Hank Penza. Hank had strong opinions about his bar. As he told a reporter, "stockbrokers, investment brokers, [and] lawyers" were not welcome. If they made the mistake of entering Mars Bar, they were rudely greeted with threats of violence and a chorus of fuck-yous.

Mars Bar became a neighborhood favorite. Its cinder-block-and-graffiti interior matched the exterior. Its proximity to the club CBGB formed a punk triangle in the Lower East Side. An experimental theater, numerous art galleries, and music venues were nearby.

The rough environment made rent cheap. Property values were low, but values like autonomy, community, and creativity were higher. You could live there without having a full-time job. That's what attracted the artists, musicians, and others.

And then the new force of financial maximization came. The city hasn't been the same since.

From 1910 to the 1960s, the average New York City apartment rent grew from $40 to $200 a month. From the 1970s to the 2010s, rent skyrocketed from an average of $335 to $3,500 a month.

Rents increased because property values were increasing. And property values were increasing because of the growing sums that banks were lending so people could buy real estate.

As the market inflated, residents of these buildings had to pay more to keep living there. Same for the small businesses who rented their storefronts. Restaurants, dry cleaners, pizza joints, drugstores, and places like Mars Bar had to squeeze to keep up. When the leases for these mom-and-pop stores expired, many faced triple-digit-percent rent hikes. A laundromat's rent went from $7,000 to $21,000 a month. There was no way to make it work.

Long-running New York City businesses closed while the new financially maximizing landlords began dominating the city. As they did, a new kind of store entered the picture: chains.

Today, national and global chains cover New York. But their appearance in the city is a recent phenomenon.

Times Square was rezoned and overhauled in the mid-1990s. Starbucks opened in New York the same year *Friends* went on the air: 1994. The first Kmart opened in 1996. Before them, few national chains opened in New York City. Fears of high crime, high taxes, and New Yorkers rejecting them deterred many chains from trying. But after these early chains succeeded in New York in the 1990s and early 2000s, more of them started setting up shop there.

Some New Yorkers fought their arrival. They argued the chains threatened the spirit of the city. They pointed to small businesses that were mortally wounded by the new neighbors. The debate was so pervasive it was the plot of the 1998 Tom Hanks–Meg Ryan romantic comedy *You've Got Mail*.

But today not many people on either side of that original

debate can afford to live in New York. Now the executives, bankers, lawyers, and stockholders of those chains are the ones who can afford the city. In two decades a complete role reversal. The critics had a point.

In 2017 there were almost as many Subway restaurants (433) as subway stations (472) in New York. Fast-food restaurants, cell phone stores, mega drugstores, and other chains dominate the city. Not to mention the hundreds of bank branches in Manhattan alone.

In many of these storefronts where there's now a chain, there once was a small business. And probably more than one. The chain storefronts are much larger than what was there before. A new bank, for example, is often created by combining three older, smaller storefronts into one. Spaces for smaller businesses are literally disappearing to make room for bigger ones.

In 2006, the punk club CBGB was replaced by a high-end fashion retailer started by the man who invented the boxer-brief. In 2011, Mars Bar and others were replaced by the TD Bank and a luxury high-rise. In 2017, the Lower East Side, once infamous for its punk and counterculture edge, had the highest concentration of chain stores in all of New York.

In 2008, a nonprofit called the Center for an Urban Future started tracking the growth of chains in the city. For ten years straight, its annual report showed chains growing across New York. In 2018, the number declined for the first time (down 1 percent) due to the impact of e-commerce. But chains remain firmly in place in New York today. This brings risks.

"One of the real defining traits of the city that makes the city unique are our independent businesses," says Jonathan Bowles, director of the Center for an Urban Future. "It's important for the city's future that New York doesn't turn into everywhere else. If New York was just a mall town no different than anywhere else, why would tourists come?"

The values that made New York City, and the Lower East Side, what it was and sometimes still is—the autonomy and freedom it provided, the creativity it allowed, the communities people built—were pushed aside in favor of financial value.

We walk by the chains and think nothing of them. They're just part of the landscape. But they're more than that. They're evidence of how our values have changed.

THE MALL

Gentrification in cities gets headlines, but what happened and is still happening to small towns and rural communities like the one I'm from is arguably even more devastating.

I'm talking, of course, about shopping centers and shopping malls.

The rise of the mall, we're told, was a perfect confluence of events. A growing middle class, the creation of the US interstate highway system, and white flight to the suburbs sparked a sudden explosion of shopping centers and suburban growth.

While these factors play a significant role, arguably just as big a catalyst for the growth of the mall is far less known. This was a 1954 change to the tax code called "accelerated depreciation."

Starting in 1909, the US tax code allowed building owners to deduct the costs of their property's gradual wear and tear (called depreciation) from their taxes. There were no rules on how much could be written off. It was left up to businesses to decide.

This pay-what-you-want policy didn't last long. As historian Thomas Hanchett notes, by 1931 "the deductions taken for depreciation in America exceeded the total taxable net income of all corporations." It's worth reading that sentence again.

America's businesses couldn't be kept on an honor system, so Congress passed laws to do it for them. To limit tax avoidance, they set a new equation defining how much could be deducted each year.

The new rules didn't last long. A few years later, leaders from the real estate industry told Congress that the deduction needed an overhaul. Because the value of real estate went down over time, developers said, more money needed to be deducted up front to spur growth. The idea of real estate going down over time might sound crazy, but real estate prices didn't behave then the way they do now. This exact rule change helped to create that shift.

Because once the new rules were in the hands of tax attorneys, commercial real estate went from a risky investment to a no-lose tax shelter. A 1955 paper by a Federal Reserve economist said the tax change amounted to a "permanent postponement of taxes."

It worked like this: invest money to build a shopping center; write off profits as losses using accelerated depreciation to avoid paying taxes; flip the property once the write-offs are done; move your money into a new development; and repeat the loophole. Over and over again.

The tax dodge was so easy new construction was happening just so people could take advantage of it. "Profits in Losses," read the front page of a 1961 *Wall Street Journal*. The paper said the "rewards of real estate ventures appear so enticing [that] a growing segment of the public is sinking money into hotels, office buildings, apartment houses, motels, shopping centers and undeveloped land." A brochure at the time proclaimed an investment in real estate was "a play for a tax advantage."

The depreciation deduction was applicable only to new developments—not for repairing or improving existing structures. This meant that the only way to take advantage of the loophole was by building new properties, like shopping centers and strip malls. Where was there cheap, undeveloped land to build? On the outskirts of town.

America's center of gravity began to shift. By 1970, the United States had thirteen thousand shopping centers. Almost all built since the tax change, and almost all built outside town.

This was how America's sprawl was built. As a tax shelter.

CHAIN REACTIONS

The growth of suburban shopping was treated as progress. The blooming of a new kind of American prosperity. Communities were joining the name-brand big leagues.

But there was a problem with this feel-good story. The downtowns of the towns and cities that these shopping centers surrounded began to die. From 1954 to 1977, the percentage of retail in American city centers dropped by 77 percent. Many downtowns never recovered.

And then Walmart, Target, and other big-box stores came along. Because of their scale, big-box stores are able to offer lower prices and a wider selection than local, smaller stores. Consumers notice. Studies have found that new Walmart stores derive 84 percent of their sales by taking them away from existing local businesses. Another study found that the expansion of three thousand Walmart stores caused the closure of twelve thousand other stores. This consolidation has a compounding effect. When a local retailer makes money, it redistributes more than 60 percent of every dollar back to the local community. When a chain takes that dollar, 40 percent stays. The rest goes out of town.

I'm not saying chains are evil. In areas like southwest Virginia where I'm from, Walmart is one of the only ways to get a lot of things that people expect and need. But it's also true that after Walmart arrived—and especially now that Amazon has also arrived—there were fewer small businesses.

Big-box retailers are sometimes called "category killers," meaning their dominant offering will put smaller competitors out of business. This term is meant admiringly. It's also turned out to be more true than anyone imagined.

STOPPED UP

The growth of chains didn't just coincide with the decline of downtowns. It also coincided with the decline of American entrepreneurship.

We're told this is the start-up era. That in every garage someone is starting a company, making an app, planning a restaurant, or creating some new 3-D–printed technology. Disrupt or be disrupted! Or something like that.

But this isn't real. This is hype.

American entrepreneurship rates today are, per capita, half of what they were in the 1970s. You read that right: half. This is analogous to the drop in smoking rates over the same time span. Think about how many more people smoked in the 1970s than today. A similarly greater proportion of people used to be entrepreneurs, too.

Start-ups volume

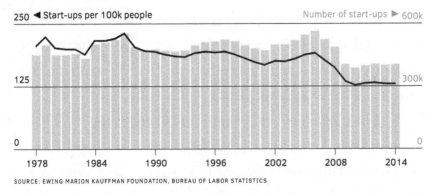

SOURCE: EWING MARION KAUFFMAN FOUNDATION, BUREAU OF LABOR STATISTICS

It's not for a lack of desire to be entrepreneurial. Two-thirds of Americans dream of starting a business. But fewer people are striking out on their own. Why? Because the threat of powerful competitors stops entrepreneurial efforts in their tracks.

How can someone start a burger joint when seven chains are already near the mall? Why open a family hardware store when Home Depot and Walmart are just outside town? Why make an app when six of the ten most-used ones are made by either Google or Facebook?

The economy is dominated by chains and market leaders that are too big, too powerful, and too aggressive to compete with. As chains have grown, businesses that were once low-hanging fruit have evolved into precise machines that are harder to take on by the day.

It's not like a new burger spot is competing against the McDonald brothers of the 1940s. It's not like a new social app is competing against Mark Zuckerberg in his dorm room. They're competing against the world's most powerful companies right now. A new company has to *start out* offering a service far better than what the market leaders offered when they first started, and as good as—if not better than—what they offer now. And just as cheap. The bar to building a successful business keeps moving higher.

The challenge of competing with large companies has created a chilling effect on entrepreneurship. Even in technology—the area where start-ups are most celebrated—entrepreneurship rates are declining.

The size of the competition is again a factor. In 2018, 70 percent of web traffic and 90 percent of digital advertising were controlled by Google and Facebook. Virtually all our mobile phone software is controlled by Apple and Google. These companies use their size to achieve unprecedented control over the web.

A significant and growing percentage of the population is reliant on these platforms for the vast majority of their personal and professional lives. Just as a significant and growing percentage of people are increasingly reliant on Amazon, Walmart, Target, and Dollar General for their necessities, jobs included. At the same time, the number of people trying to start their own business has gone down.

As the writer G. K. Chesterton put it, "Too much capitalism does not mean too many capitalists, but too few."

BIG-BOX BLIGHT

There are clear benefits to being big.

Bigger means more locations. Bigger means more name recognition. Bigger means lower prices. Bigger means having margins to reinvest into more specialized products. Bigger means being on the right side of the street at the right time of day.

These are all good things for customers and entrepreneurs. But there are also costs to this bigness. Empty downtowns. The same chains everywhere. The decline of entrepreneurship. And now empty malls.

Many of the national retailers and shopping centers that pushed small businesses to the brink in the 1990s and early 2000s are now on life support themselves. It's estimated that by 2022, more than 25 percent of malls in America will be closed.

A YouTube show called the "Dead Mall Series" documents them. "When you go into a dead mall, it's like shock and awe at the same time," the filmmaker behind it says. "That's really appealing for a lot of young people. It's like watching the *Titanic* sink."

The malls are going out of business because their scorched-earth strategy was out-scorched by internet retailers, who were able to offer even lower prices and greater convenience. The internet beat the chains at their own game.

How will this play out in the long run? Will the internet birth millions of new small businesses or will it create more consolidation than ever before? Will the internet be a city or a mall? While the internet offers seemingly infinite promise, the players keep getting bigger and attempts to maintain a level playing field, like net neutrality, have met with defeat.

And the song that took over the country charts two weeks after Sam Hunt's historic streak ended? Called "Meant to Be," it stayed #1 for fifty straight weeks, an even longer run than "Body Like a Back Road." It's the same story again and again and again and again and again and again . . .

CHAPTER FOUR

THE MULLET ECONOMY

DE-CYCLING

In 2018, America awoke to a startling new problem. The way it recycled stopped working.

In the 1980s, the practice of recycling began to grow across America. Recycling went from something few people did to something most people did. By 2013, 34 percent of America's solid waste was recycled. This growth was driven by awareness of its benefits, laws requiring its practice, and its profitability for waste management companies.

But it turns out there's a problem with how we got there.

When recycling began in the United States, it was "multi-stream." This is the industry term for when there are two or more bins for different kinds of recyclables. One for paper, one for metal, one for plastic, etc. This is how most of the world recycles.

In the 1990s and early 2000s, many American cities and towns embraced something called "single-stream" recycling: one bin for everything. With single-stream, people can throw all their recyclables into one container, and giant machines sort the different materials at the recycling plant.

The logic behind this seemed obvious: using one bin would make things more convenient, thus increasing recycling rates. (Experts differ on whether this is actually true.) Cities and waste-hauling companies were on board because single-stream recycling meant lower costs (fewer trucks, fewer drivers, fewer workers) and higher margins (more expensive trucks, more expensive trash cans, more expensive sorting equipment).

Today most recycling communities in America are single-stream. But the long-term costs of single-stream are much higher than the short-term benefits. Because from the moment recycling is picked up, single-stream recycling is much more expensive. It's costlier to sort, and the quality of material is significantly worse. In multistream recycling, just 1 to 2 percent of material ends up in landfill. In single-stream recycling, between 15 and 27 percent of the material does, because it's too dirty or isn't recyclable.

This matters. As an industry report notes: "Collection is not recycling. A product is not recycled until it is made into another product."

Since modern recycling began, China has bought most of America's recyclables. Millions of tons of it were shipped across the Pacific and reintegrated into the global supply chain. American cities and waste facilities sold recycling by the cargo load to China at a profit. Everybody won.

But those days appear to be over thanks to the messiness of America's single-stream recycling.

In 2018, China raised its standards for the recycling it would buy. According to the new rules, only 0.5 percent of it can end up in landfill. The previous year around 20 percent of the material the United States sent to China was discarded. In 2019 China refused to buy any of it. In the immediate aftermath there were reports of American cities burning their recycling because they didn't know what else to do.

The strategy created to maximize recycling collection has, for now, defeated its purpose. The failure was a group effort. Waste haulers took too many shortcuts. Communities made long-term decisions based on short-term factors. And we stopped cleaning and sorting our recycling properly.

We thought somebody else would take care of these things. For a while, trash sorters in China did. But thanks to our short-sightedness, that option appears to be gone. Said one waste facility owner about the situation: "We're our own worst enemies."

THE REVOLUTION WILL BE FINANCIALLY MAXIMIZED

In 1970 the most famous economist in the world introduced financial maximization to the mainstream.

His name was Milton Friedman. He was a star lecturer at the

University of Chicago, a future Nobel Prize winner, and future adviser to Margaret Thatcher and Ronald Reagan. He was and remains one of the most influential economists and thinkers in the world.

Nothing Friedman had shared before caught the attention of the business community quite like his 1970 op-ed in the *New York Times* that made the case for financial maximization.

At the time, the United States was mired in Vietnam. Young men were losing their lives in the war. New movements like Ralph Nader's consumer safety advocacy were demanding companies be held accountable to the public interest. What more could America's companies do for the greater good?

Milton Friedman wrote in the *New York Times* that this movement had it all wrong. To say that a company owes anything to society is absurd, he suggested. A company is not a real person, and so it cannot have any real responsibility. Furthermore, what is this responsibility you speak of? It has no definition.

If Friedman had gone on to challenge his fellow economists to define social responsibility, history might have turned out differently. But Friedman went the opposite route.

Friedman called movements for "social responsibility" (a phrase he writes in skeptical quotes twenty-three times) a "fundamentally subversive doctrine." Anyone who tried to tell someone else what to do with their money was tyrannical. Anti-freedom.

"The social responsibility of a business is profit," he thundered, turning the argument back on itself. A business exists to do what its owners—the shareholders, according to Friedman—ask it to do. And that, very simply, was to make as much money as possible.

All around America's boardrooms, dozing heads jerked up.

THE MAXIMIZING CLASS

Friedman's essay didn't cause business owners to immediately wake up with a whole new worldview. Robert Dunder, the community-minded paper supplier, didn't read the *New York Times* and suddenly decide to crush Robert Mifflin, his competitor across town.

The change was bigger and more gradual than that. A new regime was born.

They were accountants, lawyers, and consultants. They were educated at Harvard Business School, Stanford, and Wharton. They worked at Bain, Boston Consulting Group, and McKinsey. They were experts trained in the art of extracting wealth and minimizing costs. They charged outrageous rates for their advice while putting zero skin in the game themselves.

They were the Maximizing Class.

True believers in the Friedman doctrine, the Maximizing Class represented a new force in business and society with one single goal: to maximize profitability.

As growth slowed and companies stumbled during a series of downturns in the 1970s, members of the Maximizing Class were invited by boards of directors to update their companies for the new, financially maximizing age. The way these companies operated began to change. Profits grew through tax avoidance, political lobbying, and decreased quality of service. Costs were cut by freezing wages, slashing budgets, and mass firings. A book on the consulting firm McKinsey notes that "there is a distinct possibility that McKinsey may be the single greatest legitimizer of mass layoffs . . . in modern history."

The Maximizing Class advised companies to balance these smaller workforces with increased rules and processes. The number of hoops customers had to jump through went up while the support staff head count went down. Despite the poorer level of service, profits rose from increased margins.

Businesses disengaged as corporate citizens. Earlier commitments to community leadership and public service were deprioritized in favor of political donations to politicians who promised tax cuts, the removal of regulatory barriers, and, of course, more tax cuts. Influence was more efficient and effective this way.

The Maximizing Class didn't enter just businesses. Its members consulted for governments and schools, too. Their mission was to minimize expenses and maximize the money. Anyone who wasn't on board with the new strategy got marginalized or pushed out. Who made decisions began to change.

If you owned a small business, you competed with national chains who wanted to shut you down for a bump in their numbers.

If you were an engineer or scientist committed to the principles of math and science rather than how they could be financially rewarding, you had less influence than you used to.

If you were a thoughtful politician but not a great fund-raiser, you lost after being outadvertised by your opponent.

Once the goal became financial maximization, money called the shots. Everyone else got in line. Only the Maximizing Class and their overseers had decision-making privileges.

People who would have gone into other fields started joining the Maximizing Class instead. In 1970, 25,000 people in the United States graduated with a master's degree in business administration. In 2018, 200,000 people got an MBA. Our choices reflected our new values.

THE END OF RAISES

Three years after Milton Friedman's *New York Times* essay put financial maximization into the bloodstream, a strange thing happened. People stopped getting raises.

Not everybody stopped getting raises. The bosses still got them. But for pretty much everyone else, pay stopped growing. It's mostly stayed that way in the fifty years since.

Change in productivity vs. change in hourly compensation

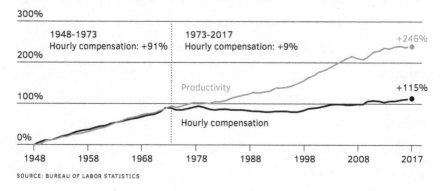

SOURCE: BUREAU OF LABOR STATISTICS

From 1948 to 1973, American hourly compensation grew 91 percent.

From 1973 to 2013, American hourly compensation grew just 9.2 percent.

Workers didn't suddenly become less productive in the 1970s. Just the opposite. People have produced more value than ever over the last half century. They've just gotten paid as if they haven't.

The high point for the American worker in terms of pay for productivity was 1973. The same year Pink Floyd's *Dark Side of the Moon* came out. It's been that long since workers have made real gains.

This isn't the case for every part of the workforce. The top earners saw their hourly wage climb 27 percent between 1979 and 2016. But for the middle class it grew just 3 percent over those same years. Just 3 percent since the Walkman was invented, and as other costs have skyrocketed.

Historians frequently point to the decline in unions and rise of globalization as catalysts for this stagnation. Once unions could no longer force companies to increase wages, raises slowed. And once companies learned how to pay people even less by shipping jobs offshore, they did that, too.

But why did those forces become so powerful? What was pushing *them*?

It was their belief in financial maximization. The goal wasn't to build a better future, raise the standard of living, or serve the needs of the public. It was to financially maximize right now. Our new hidden default.

. . . .

Just as families were struggling with newly stagnant wages in the 1970s, a miraculous new savior appeared. It was called the credit card.

The first credit card appeared in 1950. But the uptake was small. In 1966, there was effectively zero credit card debt in America. Financing life through debt was not yet a mainstream idea.

But as incomes stopped growing in the 1970s, families started reaching for credit cards. By 1980, Americans carried almost $55 billion in credit card debt. By 2018, it was $1 trillion.

When we add credit card debt to the falling incomes of American workers, we can see what's happened.

Change in productivity and compensation vs. outstanding credit card balance per US household

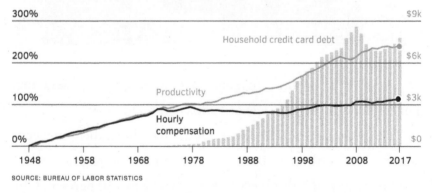

SOURCE: BUREAU OF LABOR STATISTICS

This is where the pay raises went. They became debt.

It makes sense from the Maximizing Class's perspective. The goal is financial growth. Why pay people money when you can create new money and make people borrow it with interest?

So we stopped getting raises. We started getting credit cards instead.

THE MULLET ECONOMY

When I visualize what the Maximizing Class is doing, the strangest image comes to mind. I picture a mullet. Remember the mullet? It's the hairstyle that looks like this:

A mullet is "business in front, party in back," goes the saying. The mullet was the pinnacle of 1980s hair technology.

The Maximizing Class's strategy is like the mullet, only economic. Cost-cutting/business in front for most of the population, and financial windfalls/party in back for the top 10 percent. One group's earnings and influence get cut while the other's grows. That's the Mullet Economy.

There are two steps to the Mullet Economy.

Step one is for companies to cut costs through wage freezes, layoffs, and service reductions. This is the business-in-front part of the mullet. This is what the Maximizing Class advises companies to do.

Step two is to redistribute the "saved" cash to executives and shareholders. This ensures that management gets "buy-in" (one of those phrases that accidentally tells the truth) with the board, shareholders, and public markets. This is the party in back.

It sounds simple, but the combination of these two steps has worked economic miracles. Millions of dollars that would have been paid to previously employed workers were redistributed to executives and shareholders as dividends and buybacks instead. Because getting cash is something that investors unsurprisingly like, the stock price of companies that do this tends to go up.

The most common way for companies to distribute profits today is through an instrument called a buyback. A buyback is when a company uses its cash to buy its own stock back from shareholders. When the company makes the purchase, the company's money goes to the shareholder and the shareholder's stock goes back to the company. This reduces the number of shares left in the market, and can increase a public company's stock price at the same time.

Buybacks are both common and commonly demonized today. But on their own they aren't a bad thing. Buybacks are simply a tool for companies to distribute their money.

While I was CEO at Kickstarter, we used buybacks to distribute profits to shareholders and employees. Because Kickstarter won't sell or go public, buybacks and dividends are the company's best options for sharing the financial rewards of the company's work with the employees and shareholders who helped create it and who support it today. But before doing this, we went to great effort to ensure that all eligible employees were shareholders, even going so far as to make loans to help employees exercise their options and pay the required taxes.

Buybacks themselves aren't a problem. The problems are how and why they're being used.

PROBLEM 1: WHY SOME BUYBACKS ARE HAPPENING

Up until the early 1980s, stock buybacks were illegal in the United States except in very specific circumstances. Because companies had been known to buy their own stock to drive up its price in the past, buybacks were seen as a form of stock manipulation. But in 1982—the same year that radio was opened up for business—the rules governing buybacks changed, and companies were newly allowed to purchase their own stock from investors.

Three years later, *Fortune* analyzed the stock performance of some of the early companies to do this. *Fortune*'s findings were clear: "shareholders in the buyback companies earned superb returns, far exceeding those accruing to investors as a whole."

Warren Buffett's quote in the story was the icing on the cake.

"All managements say they're acting in the shareholders' interests," he observed. "What you'd like to do as an investor is hook them up to a machine and run a polygraph to see whether it's true." Buffett said that's what a stock buyback effectively did.

The use of buybacks took off.

Aggregate stock buybacks by US firms, 1980–1990

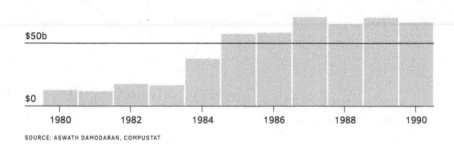

SOURCE: ASWATH DAMODARAN, COMPUSTAT

Since 1982, the practice has grown considerably. In 2018, companies paid out more than $1 trillion in buybacks, the most in history.

Aggregate stock buybacks by US firms, 1980–2018

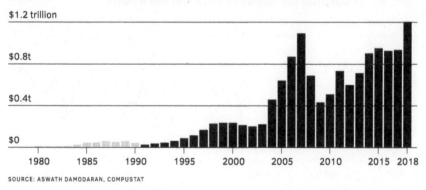

SOURCE: ASWATH DAMODARAN, COMPUSTAT

And since the buyback phenomenon began, the stock market's performance has directly reflected how much cash companies have distributed to investors through buybacks and dividends.

S&P 500 quarterly dividends and buybacks, annualized

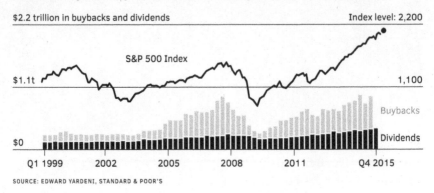

$2.2 trillion in buybacks and dividends   Index level: 2,200

S&P 500 Index

$1.1t   1,100

Buybacks

$0   Dividends

Q1 1999   2002   2005   2008   2011   Q4 2015

SOURCE: EDWARD YARDENI, STANDARD & POOR'S

This is an economy dutifully following the expectations of financial maximization. The goal is to maximize returns for shareholders. In recent years, many American companies have invested less in R&D than they've spent on stock buybacks.

Net share buybacks and net capital formation as a share of net operation surplus for nonfinancial corporations

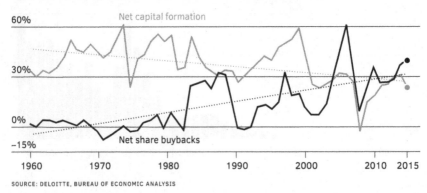

60%   Net capital formation

30%

0%

−15%   Net share buybacks

1960   1970   1980   1990   2000   2010 2015

SOURCE: DELOITTE, BUREAU OF ECONOMIC ANALYSIS

This isn't something companies do everywhere. The *Financial Times* reports that, "Between 2015 and 2017, the five biggest US tech groups (especially Apple and Microsoft) spent $228 billion on stock buybacks and dividends, Bloomberg data shows. During the same period, the top five Chinese tech companies spent just $10.7 billion and ploughed the rest of their excess cash into investments that broaden their footprint and influence."

Which sounds like the better strategy to you?

PROBLEM 2: WHO'S LEFT OUT

When the buyback rules changed in the early 1980s, the United States was in a recession that saw 9 percent of workers lose their jobs in layoffs. It was the highest rate since the Great Depression. Jobs and factories were disappearing in droves.

Companies said they needed to tighten their belts to stay competitive. But this belt tightening didn't apply to the people in charge. Money that was going to workers started going to investors and management instead. The mullet began, and has continued to grow since.

Yahoo spent $6.6 billion on buybacks between 2008 and 2014 as the company laid off workers and spiraled toward irrelevance. The fading retailer Sears spent more than $6 billion on buybacks after 2005 while workers lost their jobs. Yahoo and Sears spent—and arguably wasted—billions of dollars buying their own stock (billions of dollars in shares of companies in existential trouble, as they knew better than anyone) to please shareholders. More than employees, customers, or its own future, shareholders and the stock price were the priority.

It's important to note that a shareholder-centric economy is, practically speaking, a wealth-centric economy. Eighty percent of stocks are owned by the richest 10 percent of Americans. The bottom 80 percent of the population owns just 8 percent of stocks. Companies spending billions on buybacks are primarily redistributing their profits to the richest 10 percent of the population.

The problem here isn't shareholders being wealthy or investors benefiting from their investments. The problem is workers have a direct hand in the success of these companies, and yet they've been rewarded with frozen wages and mass layoffs. Companies are producing bigger profits than ever, yet workers are meant to count themselves lucky for having a job at all. While shareholders enjoy record returns, workers' pay is stagnant and their jobs are increasingly insecure.

The rewards of our economy are bypassing workers and going straight to shareholders on top, while the costs bypass shareholders and fall on the shoulders of everyone else. That's the Mullet Economy.

PROBLEM 3: WHAT THIS MEANS FOR THE FUTURE

In May 2018, the Federal Reserve Bank of Dallas hosted a conference on the impact of automation on companies and workers.

In one panel discussion, the moderator asked a group of CEOs whether they could envision "broad-based wage gains again" for their workers in the future. The panel was clear: no.

"It's just not going to happen," the CEO of the Coca-Cola franchise in Florida responded. "Absolutely not in my business."

The same CEO said that his company was hiring people that they knew they would eventually lay off because of shifts to automation. It was the inevitable future of their business.

This is how corporations are thinking about the future: automation and robots are in, human beings are out. This is the future they're investing in. It's just rational business.

This is the real problem with the Mullet Economy: what it means for an automation-based future.

In a world dominated by financial maximization, companies are expected to minimize costs and maximize financial returns. But what happens when this expectation combines with automated workforces, and the spoils of the global economy are only reaped and sown by the world's largest companies and their small band of very wealthy shareholders?

This would be a world with more profits and fewer workers than we can possibly imagine. Where stock buybacks—or whatever their future equivalent might be—are through the roof and inequality along with it. This would be a world of "profits without prosperity," as the economist William Lazonick has put it.

Our current trajectory is driving us toward this future in Insane Mode, while keeping us woefully unprepared for the shocks that will come when we get there.

We need a better answer for what to do with excess capital than give it away to shareholders. One potential answer is higher taxes combined with some version of a universal basic income. This has merits and challenges too long to go into here. Regardless of the specific plan, if we don't change course we'll end up in an ugly future with a very big mullet.

MULLET UNIVERSITY

Some of the biggest victims of the Mullet Economy aren't even part of it yet. They're college students, soon-to-be college students, and recent college graduates who are taking on record amounts of debt to enter the workforce.

Why are they victims of the Mullet Economy? Because at the same time pay has stagnated, the cost of higher education has gone through the roof. The average college tuition in 2018 is nineteen times bigger than it was in 1971. From $1,832 in 1971 (using today's dollars) to $34,740 today.

To make up the difference, students have turned to another kind of credit card: student loans. As of 2018, more than $1.4 trillion in student debt is outstanding in the United States, up 150 percent in the past ten years.

But many of those debt holders are having trouble keeping up. Nearly a third of borrowers are in default or forbearance. They don't make enough money to pay back their debts and all the other costs of life. The cost of college and necessities went up, but wages did not.

Unlike debt-fueled start-ups, real estate developers, and other businesses, students are legally barred from filing bankruptcy to escape their debts. In fact, some in Congress have even proposed instituting mandatory garnishment of future wages to collect what students borrowed.

The financial maximizers escape this. They have the money to pay for tuition. They don't take on debt. It's those from outside the Maximizing Class who pay the biggest price. Their pay is kept down, but the cost of the right to earn that pay keeps going up.

This is a significant problem if you're one of those students, but not if you're one of their future employers. Debt-addled students are more likely to be future worker bees than risk-taking entrepreneurs and challengers to the status quo. Their student loan payments will depend on it.

THE POLITICAL ECONOMY

If things don't change, the world will stay the same.

For some parts of life that sounds pretty great. For others it sounds horribly depressing. Those areas differ for each of us.

It's the same for society. While some people push for a different future, others try to make sure the future resembles the present. The competition between those views is handled in many arenas, politics being the most important arena of all.

Politics is the explicit competition to determine society's norms and rules. Which way should we go? Which idea is right? Elections and political debate are how those choices are meant to be made.

But because of money, this competition is rarely a fair fight.

The path of politics and money is like what happened with recycling. We once lived in a world where politics and money were more separate. They were multistream. But today money and politics are single-stream. And like recycling, politics has become so dirty it's stopped serving its actual purpose.

A startling research paper from three political scientists in 2015 showed that elections are decided almost entirely by money.

In "results that surprised even us," the researchers found that "in three widely spaced years—1980, when Congress functioned very differently than it does today, 1996, and 2012—the relation between major party candidates' shares of the two party vote and their proportionate share of total campaign expenditures were strongly linear—more or less straight lines, in fact."

After running additional studies on every congressional election between 1980 and 2014, they found a direct ratio between the amount of money a candidate spent and how large a share of the vote he or she received.

"For every 1% increase in the money split compared to the other party's," they write, "the vote is expected to increase by 1.277%."

For every extra dollar a candidate spends versus their opponent, the candidate's share of the vote increases an equal amount. The analysis shows that every US congressional election between 1980 and 2014 except one fit this model.

The same researchers collated a variety of sources on political giving to see where this money came from. They found that most of the money came from the largest corporations, their executives, and the top 1 percent of wealthiest Americans. The Maximizing Class and the wealthiest of the wealthy are the dominant force in American politics.

Remember those graphs from earlier showing how congressional reelection rates have risen even as disapproval rates have, too? This is why that's happening. By outspending the competition, the Maximizing Class keeps friendly politicians in office and a financially maximizing force inside government.

In exchange for the contributions, politicians have acted like wrecking balls working on behalf of private companies inside government. They've weakened unions, watered down pollution laws, expanded tax loopholes, deregulated industries, and undercut as much of the government as the people writing the checks have asked. When the politicians leave office, plum lobbying jobs await them.

Financial maximization would not be the force it is without its political influence. The Mullet Economy was enabled by regulatory changes achieved through political—not business—means. Stock buybacks were prohibited until friendly regulators allowed them in 1982.

In the 1980s and 1990s numerous restrictions on banks were removed, including prohibitions on banks having branches in multiple states (this change was key to the bank branch takeover of New York City). In 1999 a bill was signed into law that removed long-standing restrictions on the size and operations of banks that had been in place since the Great Depression. The deregulatory changes contributed to multiple financial crises (including

Enron and the 2008 housing crisis) within a decade of their passing.

These changes were made possible by the political donations and influence of the Maximizing Class. Financial maximization was the underlying motive behind all of these changes. The rational choice was whichever option made the most money. That was what mattered.

THE ENTREPRENEURIAL STATE

It's common belief today that government and private companies are like Tom and Jerry: natural enemies. But this hasn't always been the case.

In her illuminating book *The Entrepreneurial State*, the economist Mariana Mazzucato shows how deeply connected government and private companies have been, and how beneficial those relationships have proven to be.

As an example, Mazzucato demonstrates that the technology behind every part of the iPhone—from the touch screen to 3G wireless to GPS to the internet itself—was directly funded by the US government. Apple brilliantly commercialized the technology, but the work behind the iPhone was created by academic researchers funded by federal investments.

The work goes back decades. After the Second World War, the United States began investing heavily in research in science, technology, medicine, and other fields through the Defense Advanced Research Projects Agency, or DARPA. This agency is in charge of identifying and funding technologies that could provide military and domestic benefits.

Over the years DARPA marked everything from computer programming languages to jet technology to GPS as areas for investment. It funded new computer science programs at leading engineering schools to train promising students in these new concepts.

The internet began as a DARPA project. The very first computer network, called ARPANET, was created in 1967 and funded with $1 million from a ballistic missile defense budget. Over time ARPANET evolved into the internet that we use today, most of it paid for with farsighted public funds. And now we can all tweet about how wasteful government spending is.

Even some of the leading technology companies—including Intel and Apple—received assistance from extraordinarily successful government grants and loans created to spark the field of computer technology.

This sounds impossible to today's mind-set. Apple, the same company that parks money offshore to avoid billions in taxes, took start-up money from the US government? That wasn't in the movie. We think government blocks progress and innovation comes from people like Steve Jobs fighting it.

That's the story now, but in the recent past private and public interests were aligned behind an ambitious vision of the future. The government funded farsighted research that private companies commercially developed. Americans participated as workers and beneficiaries of the discoveries they helped make. Corporate and personal tax dollars were invested into the next generations of innovation. This arrangement produced some of the most significant technological leaps in human history and many of the benefits we enjoy today.

This is the same strategy that financial maximizers have spent so much money in political donations to destroy. Extensive lobbying for tax cuts and cutting of government spending has resulted in decreased investments in long-term research. Despite the tremendous returns it has produced, federal spending on R&D as a percentage of the federal budget has declined since some of these significant investments were made.

It's exactly this kind of spending that the Maximizing Class, corporate lobbyists, and their politicians have sought to dismantle.

Why? If direct government investments were so successful in the past, why do America's largest companies and wealthiest people want to defund them now? Especially when many of these same people and their companies—tech companies, pharmaceutical companies, and others—owe the foundations of their success to research funded by these same programs in the past?

For some it's simple financial maximization. Companies will never stop fighting for more of the pie. Others want government doing as little as possible, both to keep taxes down and to keep the market as open as possible.

But I think there's another reason, too. These companies know firsthand how much of an impact this kind of research can have. For a company that's already dominant, future scientific breakthroughs are one of the few potential existential threats they face. A breakthrough drug or technology can change the playing field. As long as everything stays the same or they're the ones doing the discovering, they've got nothing to worry about.

Now that the financial rewards from decades of government investments are being realized, companies are staking their claim on as much as they can. All while starving the government of the resources it needs to seed the next generation of innovation by hiding money in tax shelters and lobbying for tax cuts.

Mazzucato makes a convincing argument that we should think of government funding as investment rather than spending. If we viewed the returns on these funds like a business would, we would think very differently about public funding, and be happy with what we found. Some notable failed government investments—Concorde in the UK and Solyndra in the United States—are often brought up to say that government should stay out of the private sector. But those losses are peanuts compared to the successes, and of course private investors aren't considered failures if they make a bad bet. Government investments are held to an impossible standard in a bid to maintain the status quo.

This is called pulling the ladder up behind you.

THE DEAD END

In 1972, the CEOs of some of America's largest corporations formed a group called the Business Roundtable. Their mission was to lobby for pro-business policies in government. With the implicit endorsement of America's biggest companies behind them, the group's recommendations carry a lot of weight.

So when the group made a significant shift in how they defined a company's responsibilities during the 1980s and 1990s, this mattered. National Medal of Science–winning mathematician Ralph Gomory observes:

"In 1981, the Business Roundtable wrote in its Statement on Corporate Responsibility that companies should always consider the effects their actions have on a number of groups including their shareholders, their communities, their employees, and society at large. But by 1997, their Statement on Corporate Governance discussed only how they could best serve their shareholders."

Employees, communities, and society at large were no longer a priority. Only shareholders were.

The hyperfocus on financial maximization took off with Milton Friedman's argument for the virtue of profits, and grew as Wall Street and others normalized these expectations. As the economist Mariana Mazzucato writes, "The return on financial sector investment sets a minimum for the return on 'real' fixed investment, a floor which rises as financial operations become more portable. Non-financial companies that cannot beat the financial investors' return are forced to join them by 'financializing' their production distribution activities." In other words, even if a company wasn't financially maximizing before, once investors started expecting those kinds of returns companies had to follow along.

Financial maximization and a shareholder-centric view of the world soon became our new default.

In the half century of financial maximization since, profits and GDP have soared. But the rewards of that growth have only been shared with some, creating challenging problems if we project these same strategies into our likely future. Especially if we consider financial maximization's playbook once it's calling the shots. It has four phases.

PHASE 1: THE END OF COMPETITION

The end of competition begins with the industry's major players consolidating. Small and regional players are forced to sell or go out of business. Swaths of the industry or geographic territories are carved up and split between the remaining companies. Big players become even bigger players. National chains take over. Eventually direct competition all but disappears.

Sometimes, like in the case of radio, laws meant to preserve competition must be removed before consolidation can take place. After political donations ensure that the right politicians are "bought in," the changes are sold to the public by claiming that the decreased regulations will spur innovation and growth. In reality, they'll spur lots of financial growth for a tiny percentage of the population.

PHASE 2: MASS LAYOFFS

Once companies stop worrying about competing with each other, mass firings and budget cuts begin.

All manner of vernacular has been created to describe mass firings: achieving efficiencies, eliminating redundancies, finding synergies. A lot of thousand-dollar phrases that imply these decisions are some deeply strategic brilliance.

The reality is much more basic. The more that budgets can be cut and jobs can be eliminated, the more money executives can redistribute to investors and themselves. They've done a bang-up job of it. Since 1977, median wages have budged barely 10 percent while executive compensation has soared 1,000 percent.

PHASE 3: EXTRACT AND DISTRIBUTE

With workers and competitors out of the picture, the mind-set changes from the pursuit of excellence in that industry to extracting money from that industry. The quality of service gets worse, and the profit margins increase. Cases in point: cable and internet providers in America, and radio stations' shrinking playlists. The newly saved funds are distributed to shareholders through stock buybacks and dividends while service stagnates. Or, as we call it, the Mullet Economy.

PHASE 4: THE CRASH

Once value extraction is maximized, it's only a matter of time before whatever goodwill the company has left is gone. Think of Yahoo and Sears paying out billions of dollars to shareholders while their businesses crumbled.

You might think this is a problem for financial maximization. If it all ends in a crash, what good is it?

Truthfully, it doesn't matter. The investments that started the cycle cashed out long ago. That money is already on to the next thing. By the time of the crash phase, third, fourth, and fifth generations of money are involved, everyone extracting whatever they can and leaving employees and their communities to fend for themselves. The people on top still get paid and the money keeps moving.

Financial maximization is a never-ending search for costs to cut and value to extract. Even in periods of success, its only move is to downsize people and redistribute money to shareholders. There's no vision for anything else. There's only this. Financial maximization isn't a plan. It's a trap.

CHAPTER FIVE

THE TRAP

I WAS STANDING IN LINE AT THE GROCERY STORE WHEN THE magazine caught my eye. The cover was splashed with red, yellow, and a list of menacing phrases.

"Be paranoid."

"Disrupt yourself."

"Go to war."

Was this *Guns & Ammo*? The *National Enquirer*? *Adbusters*?

It was *Harvard Business Review*.

At the time I was Kickstarter's CEO. I'd been one of the company's cofounders and leaders for nearly a decade. But in the time since I'd taken the CEO seat almost two years before, Kickstarter had grown to more than one hundred employees. What had been an exciting adventure felt more serious by the day.

To the outside world, we were a big success. In 2013, the leading tech site TechCrunch nominated Kickstarter for "Best

Overall Startup" alongside Twitter, Uber, Snapchat, and Cloud-flare. Despite being by far the smallest nominee by team size, Kickstarter won.

But inside myself, I struggled with anxiety. The pressure I felt was immense. Creative people relied on our tool to fund their ideas. Employees and families relied on the company for their livelihood. There was a reputation to protect. Investors and competitors to think about. Hundreds of millions of dollars that changed hands through our system each year. Daily opportunities for things to go wrong.

The weight never left. At home, on weekends, with my family, even in dreams. What wasn't I worried about that I should be worried about? There was no off switch.

My darkest fear was always the same. That an unforeseen

event would blow it up because I failed to do something that a better CEO would know to do. This was my RAM fear always running in the background: that I didn't measure up.

So as I stood in line at the grocery store, the *Harvard Business Review* cover touched a nerve.

Be paranoid. Disrupt yourself. Go to war.

Maybe that's my problem, I thought. *I'm not paranoid* enough.

I put the magazine in my cart.

LIFE GOALS

Since 1966, researchers at UCLA's Higher Education Research Institute have conducted the nation's largest study on the attitudes of America's college students.

Each year, the CIRP Freshman survey asks incoming college students the same questions about their backgrounds, habits, and values. To date, 15 million freshmen across the United States have answered them.

One question asks students to rate potential life goals. Students are given a list of about a dozen choices to rate as essential, very important, somewhat important, or not important.

When the survey was administered to incoming freshmen in 1967, the life goals most named by freshmen as "essential" or "very important" were to:

1. Develop a meaningful philosophy of life (85% saying this was essential or very important)

2. Be an authority in my field (70%)

3. Help others in difficulty (63%)

4. Keep up to date with political affairs (54%)

5. Become successful in a business of my own (44%)

And lower down:

7. Be very well off financially (41%)

In 1970, incoming freshmen answered:

1. Develop a meaningful philosophy of life (79%)

2. Help others in difficulty (74%)

3. Raise a family (72%)

4. Have friends different than me (65%)

5. Be an authority in my field (60%)

And much lower:

13. Be very well off financially (28%)

Starting in the mid-1970s, students' answers began to change.

After a steady climb in the 1970s and 1980s, "Be very well off financially" became the most "essential" or "very important" life goal for the first time in 1989. This group, the college class of 1993, was born around 1970—the same year Milton Friedman's essay ran in the *New York Times*. They'd grown up in a world where financial maximization was normal. Their aspirations—and the aspirations of every class that has followed them—reflected this. "Be very well off financially" has been the top goal almost every year since.

Here's how incoming freshmen responded in 2016:

1. Be very well off financially (82%)
2. Help others who are in difficulty (77%)
3. Raise a family (71%)
4. Improve my understanding of other countries and cultures (59%)
5. Become an authority in my field (58%)
6. Influence social values (48%)

And lower:

8. Develop a meaningful philosophy of life (46%)

Since 1970, the goal of being rich went from essential for 28 percent of college freshmen to 82 percent of college freshmen. The largest change in score among any of the options. At the same time, the goal of developing a meaningful philosophy of life dropped by almost half.

In the 1960s, four out of five college freshmen thought having a purpose in life was essential. In 2016, four out of five college freshmen already knew what their purpose in life was: to be rich.

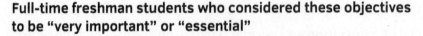

Full-time freshman students who considered these objectives to be "very important" or "essential"

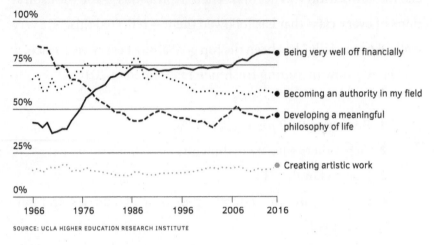

SOURCE: UCLA HIGHER EDUCATION RESEARCH INSTITUTE

The attitudes among America's best and brightest radically changed. "In 1965 only 11% of Harvard Business School MBAs went into the financial sector," writes economist Mariana Mazzucato. "By 1985 the figure had reached 41% and has risen since." Year by year, class by class, our belief in financial maximization grew.

ROLE MODELS

Founder of capitalism Adam Smith wrote that the "disposition to admire, and almost to worship, the rich and the powerful and to despise, or, at least, to neglect persons of poor and mean condition" was "necessary both to establish and to maintain the distinction of ranks and the order of society."

In other words, a culture's role models set its values. Both in who it celebrates and who it doesn't.

In the world of business and innovation, the role models are clear. They're successful rich people. People who achieved their dreams, forced their enemies (yes, enemies) to fail at theirs, and made hundreds of millions of dollars doing it. While you're doing chores on a Saturday, they're learning Mandarin and inspiring their employees to work through the holiday weekend. "Aye-aye!" the team responds in smiling unison to the CEO's face on the screens above.

As absurd as this sounds, images like these influence our definitions of success. If only I was richer. If only I was more successful. If only I was more like them and less like me.

But whether it's what you look like, how you rank versus your peers, or how much money you have, basing your self-worth on external validation does not turn out well.

We imagine these external goals as destinations. Once we reach them everything will be okay. The moment we get the big promotion there will be a sitcom freeze-frame while the credits start rolling. Congratulations on winning at life! There's nothing to worry about anymore ever!

That's not how it works. Instead, by the time you get to what you thought was the Promised Land, a voice will shout, "No, wait, it's over here!" and you'll start all over again trying to get somewhere else. Even as you run your own company you may find yourself fear-buying a business magazine at a grocery store.

Another study of life goals and college students hints at why. Experts in motivation at the University of Rochester asked students about their life goals, much like the CIRP study discussed earlier. But this time, researchers followed up with students one and two years later to see whether they'd achieved their goals, and how they felt about them.

The researchers found that people whose life goals were "extrinsic"—meaning external goals like wealth, physical appearance, or recognition—were less satisfied by achieving those goals than people whose goals were "intrinsic"—focused on learning, improving, or helping others. Achieving "profit goals," as researchers called them, was less satisfying than achieving "purpose goals."

For those who achieved profit goals, success didn't make them happier. In fact, they showed increased anxiety and depression. When more money fails to satisfy, we increase our financial goals, thinking that will fix the problem. It doesn't.

Our desire for satisfaction exceeds the satisfaction of satisfaction. As we get more, we want more. When our expectations go up for profit-oriented goals, this leads to an insatiable hunger to be more attractive, get more recognition, or make more money. All of which are powerful motivators that provide only fleeting relief. But when our expectations go up for purpose-oriented goals— like wanting to be better at our profession, wanting to know more about a subject, or wanting better relationships—that drive produces fruitful and lasting outcomes: a calling, steps toward mastery, and a stronger community around you.

When we base our ideas of success on external motivators,

we enter a race without a finish line. There's no winning, only the race.

SCARED SUCCESSFUL

During the Internet 2.0 era—which spanned about ten years and ended with the 2016 US presidential election—fast growth and big valuations defined the mainstream idea of success.

In 2014, a *New York Times* article profiled an HR software start-up called Zenefits, which, the lead sentence explains, is "one of the fastest-growing companies in recent Silicon Valley history." The profile glowingly notes the company's fast growth, A-list Silicon Valley investors, and a recent $4.5 billion "unicorn" valuation. Zenefits was the newest zeitgeist-shaking success.

But in the article, Zenefits' founder and CEO, a man named Parker Conrad, gives a series of startling quotes that clash with the breathless tone. While the *Times* and investors quoted in the article celebrate the company's growth, here's how Conrad describes it:

"Even when we think things are going well, it always feels like the wheels are ready to come off the cart."

And: "The problems that other companies have a year to figure out, we have like eight weeks . . . It's incredibly scary. I feel like it takes years off my life."

"Mr. Conrad often finds himself petrified, his days a series of white-knuckled attempts to escape the clutches of sudden, inadvertent failure," writes the *Times*.

Success means disrupting an industry and becoming a unicorn

all before breakfast. The fact that someone with that success was publicly crying for help in the *New York Times* was ignored. It was easier to believe the image we'd been presented than the reality right in front of us. This is perfectly encapsulated in the story's headline: "Zenefits' Leader Is Rattling an Industry, So Why Is He Stressed Out?"

Why was Conrad stressed? Because Zenefits was a quickly growing service that aggressively raised nearly half a billion dollars in venture capital money based on that growth, and then had to keep delivering those growth rates—or better—for the foreseeable future. A year later Conrad was fired for violating state regulations to keep it up. The *Times* reported that the company's board members had been pushing for faster growth.

Though extreme, the story of Zenefits is not unusual. To fulfill the hyperexpectations that investors and others have, people run themselves ragged and take dubious shortcuts to get there. Many of the story lines on the HBO series *Silicon Valley* are built on this based-on-a-true-story premise.

Here's how the cofounder and ex-CEO of another celebrated "fastest-growing company ever," Andrew Mason, formerly of Groupon, put it:

> Groupon started out with these really tight principles about how the site was going to work, really being pro-customer. And as we expanded people in the company would say, "Hey, why don't we try running two deals a day?" "Why don't we start sending two emails a day?" And I'd think, *That sounds*

awful. Who wants to get two emails every single day from a company. And they'd be like, *Sure, it sounds awful to you. But we're a data-driven company, so why don't we let the data decide? Why don't we do a test?* And we'd do a test, and it would show that maybe people would unsubscribe at a slightly higher rate, but the increase in purchasing would more than make up for it. You'd get in a situation where it doesn't feel right, but it does seem like a rational decision.

The RAND Corporation's book on game theory defined what's rational as "to gain as much from the game as a player can, safely, in the face of a skillful opponent who is pursuing an antithetical goal." In the real world, getting as much as you can right now often comes at a long-term cost. And once growth expectations are set, that mitigating word "safely" becomes increasingly optional when it comes to gaining "as much from the game as a player can."

Early on, companies follow the path of least resistance—big money, growth at all costs, act now and think about the consequences never—before getting trapped by their choices down the line. Once a company invites the mind-set of financial maximization inside its doors, it's only a matter of time before it starts running the show.

DISRUPT YOURSELF

"Be paranoid."

"Disrupt yourself."

"Go to war."

I glanced at the unopened *Harvard Business Review* on my coffee table. *Why did I buy this?*

Finally, I opened it. What scary wisdom was about to blow my mind? The paranoia-inducing cover story was, in reality, an article by two McKinsey partners about profit margins.

I felt like the kid in *A Christmas Story* decoding "DRINK YOUR OVALTINE." *All of that—for this?*

I tossed the magazine. But at the same time I started taking note of this aggressive tone whenever I came across it in the world of business.

I started seeing it on magazine covers: This CEO is out for blood. These businesses own the world.

In headlines: The war for tech dominance. The streaming media arms race. The Great Tech War of 2012. The Great AI War. Keeping count of Silicon Valley casualties.

In news stories: Former Uber CEO Travis Kalanick's texts and emails included phrases like "war time," "burn the village," and "pound of flesh." Mark Zuckerberg was reported to have told his leaders that Facebook was at "war" after it faced criticism for its role in election interference.

In everyday business vernacular: Destroy the competition. Poach employees. Capture a market. Make a killing.

This kind of language had nothing to do with building a strong organization, making good decisions, or improving the status quo. Just the opposite. This was language of violence, conquest, and war.

As we learned with the Wall Street and Community Games, words matter. This language is telling us how to play the game.

Compete, don't cooperate. Win no matter what. Financially maximize or die. The instructions are clear, but a question is left unanswered: When we play the game this way, who wins?

. . . .

Some of these same publications that sparked my anxiety had written about me in the past as someone who had made it. You might think this would make me immune to the comparisons these ideals create. Unfortunately that's not the case.

Sure, I'd gotten this far, but I was a nobody from Clover Hollow, Virginia. Other people were the smart and successful people. I'd just gotten lucky.

When I read stories about killer CEOs who never stopped working, never stopped selling, and who lived without fear or regret, I judged myself. Yes, I worked all the time. Yes, I was always representing my company. But when I looked at myself I didn't see someone who was cutthroat. I didn't know if that was someone I could ever be.

As I held myself up to these images, I'd ask myself a very difficult question: *Can I do this job and still be me?* I wasn't sure.

I didn't want others to know my doubts. In social settings the gap was especially pronounced.

CEO at an event: "How's everything?"

Another CEO: "Amazing! Literally the best it's ever been. And it's only getting better."

Other CEO: "No way! It's the same for me!"

They turn to me: "How's everything?"

Me: "Awesome! Literally the best it's ever been. I didn't know things could be this good!"

Everyone a human PR department. I feared that if they knew what was going on in my head I'd be confirmed as the imposter they already knew I was.

I'd leave the event early and go home to work more. On my nightstand were a half dozen leadership and strategy books to cram-read each night before falling asleep, where I could dream new things to worry about. The answer to my self-doubt was out there somewhere. If I just worked hard enough, I'd find it.

NOT FOR BREAD ALONE

Even as I had my inner battles, Kickstarter was secure. From day one, Kickstarter has been a purpose-oriented company, not a profit-oriented company. We weren't interested in playing the game others were playing. We had deliberately taken ourselves out of that race.

Kickstarter was the opposite of Zenefits and Groupon. While they raised huge amounts of venture capital and set expectations for a big payday, we saw the hypergrowth path for what it was: short-term returns in exchange for long-term compromises.

Our slow and steady strategy was unlike what our peers were doing. In a period of big money and fast growth, we turned our backs on how others thought about success, striving for our own ideals and goals instead, like succeeding for the long haul as a public benefit corporation.

Still, there were moments when I doubted our course. Within a month of my taking over as CEO, two other companies in our space announced a combined $60 million in funding from top venture capitalists aiming to take us on. It was a gut-check moment. *Should we do the same?* We stuck to our course and the moment passed.

It was during my time as CEO that I came across a book that gave me newfound confidence. Called *Not for Bread Alone*, it was a series of essays from the long career of a Japanese businessman named Konosuke Matsushita.

Matsushita led an extraordinary life. In 1918, he started one of the first electrical companies in Japan, which he ran for more than forty years. That company continues to operate today under the name Panasonic. *Not for Bread Alone* shares philosophies and lessons from Matsushita's long career, which is remarkable not just for its longevity but also for its broader idea of prosperity.

Here's Matsushita addressing his employees in 1932:

"The mission of a manufacturer is to overcome poverty, to relieve society as a whole from the misery of poverty and bring it wealth. Business and production are not meant simply to enrich the shops or the factories of the enterprise concerned, but all of society. And society needs the dynamism and vitality of business and industry to generate its wealth. Only under such conditions will business and factories truly prosper."

At this same time Matsushita declared the company's 250-year goal: "the elimination of poverty from this world."

He meant it. In 1936, Matsushita decided to give his employees one day off a week at a time when Japanese workers got two days off *a month*. It wasn't until 1947 that one day off a week was official by Japanese Labor Standards Law.

In 1960, Matsushita went further, announcing that the company would offer Japan's first five-day workweek. "We need a dramatic increase in productivity if we want to compete with foreign companies," he said. "Having two days off every week will help us to achieve this by giving us ample time to refresh mind and body, and greater opportunities to enrich our lives." To produce more and to produce better, Matsushita counterintuitively proposed people work *less*. Matsushita implemented two days off a week in the 1960s, but it took until 1980 for most big Japanese firms to follow, and until 1992 for Japanese government workers to have five-day workweeks.

Matsushita was also a proud capitalist. "Only by making a reasonable profit—neither too much nor too little—can an enterprise expand and be of greater service to more people," he wrote. "Moreover, the enterprise contributes to society by paying a large portion of its profits in the form of taxes. In that sense, it is a businessperson's duty, as a citizen, to make a reasonable profit."

Matsushita named five spirits to guide the company:

1. Spirit of service through industry
2. Spirit of fairness
3. Spirit of harmony and cooperation
4. Spirit of striving for progress
5. Spirit of courtesy and humility

Almost eighty years later, many of Panasonic's offices still began their days by reading these spirits aloud.

The contrast between Matsushita's way of seeing the world and the "disrupt yourself" tone of my present day couldn't have been bigger. The words of this elderly Japanese man were transformative for me. I had a leadership role model for the first time. A foundation that gave me the confidence to trust the same instincts I'd spent so much time doubting before.

This knowledge helped me better manage my emotions—which still came, of course—and to better integrate the values-driven and business-driven parts of me. I would try to imagine how Matsushita would see a situation, looking for the vantage point that would let me see which values were most at stake. More often than not, I would learn something from the process.

Feeling more confident, I opened up to other CEOs about my anxieties. I was surprised to learn most were going through their own version of the same thing. Here I thought everyone else had it made and I was the only broken one. What an immense relief. My fears even became something I could joke about, acknowledging and letting them pass at the same time.

THE WAY OUT

We hope our anxieties will be answered by whatever our current goal is. If this next opportunity happens I'll be set. We're like the aging bank robber declaring "one more job and I'm out." But after that job is another job. And another after that. Our baseline never stops shifting. That's the trap.

How can we escape this? There's a Bible verse that tells us how: Ephesians 6:12. It reads: "For our struggle is not against flesh and blood, but against the rulers, against the authorities, against the powers of this dark world."

One more time:

"For our struggle is not against flesh and blood, but against the rulers, against the authorities, against the powers of this dark world."

In other words: Don't hate the player, hate the game.

In the financial maximization era, we're recruited into the flesh-and-blood struggle of making as much money as we can. That's the point of it all. But as we've seen, there are more fleeting victories than lasting winning in that game. Even factoring in the potential payoffs, it's a high price to pay.

Rather than losing ourselves in competition against each other, we should make sure we're playing the right game. As long as our eyes are on the flesh-and-blood struggle rather than the game itself, the rulers and authorities will remain. This is their game, after all.

■ ■ ■ ■

Financial maximization seems locked into place. An iron cage reinforced with space-age materials and an unbreakable crypto key. How it is and how it always will be.

But even it was once new.

The *New York Times* published Milton Friedman's essay in 1970 because he was a respected economist with a proposition. He was writing to persuade people that his idea had merit. Just as I, in a much more humble way, am doing now.

Selling this idea wasn't as easy as you might think. To argue in the Vietnam War era and at the height of the Cold War that companies had no social responsibility beyond profit was audacious. But with an effective argument and wide exposure, this idea became accepted. Now financial maximization is like the high five: college students can't imagine life without it.

But despite the seeming permanence of now, there's no end to history. Every destination is temporary. This isn't the end. It's just the beginning.

PART TWO

PART TWO

PART TWO

CHAPTER SIX

WHAT'S REALLY VALUABLE?

IF YOU HAD THE OPPORTUNITY TO REDESIGN YOUR LIFE, chances are you'd give yourself a raise. That doesn't make you greedy or selfish. It makes you practical. Financial security is correlated with a quality life.

These are the ten wealthiest people in the world in 2019:

1. Jeff Bezos (Amazon)
2. Bill Gates (Microsoft)
3. Warren Buffett (Berkshire Hathaway)
4. Bernard Arnault (LVMH)
5. Carlos Slim Helu (America Movil)
6. Amancio Ortega (Zara)
7. Larry Ellison (Oracle)
8. Mark Zuckerberg (Facebook)

9. Michael Bloomberg (Bloomberg LP)

10. Larry Page (Alphabet/Google)

Are these the ten happiest people in the world? Probably not. But they're probably not the ten *least* happy people either.

The costs of being not-rich are significant. Especially now. America, it's been said, is a country where luxuries are cheap and the essentials are expensive. The rising costs of health care, transportation, housing, and other necessities bear this out. Two out of every five Americans (43 percent) can't afford these things each month. Thanks to the Mullet Economy, few Americans lead a financially secure life.

People aren't crazy to base their lives around financial needs. Financial security is important. The benefits of financial security go far beyond money. Studies show that financial security is a critical threshold after which a person is more likely to be educated, healthy, and long-term oriented.

The argument against financial maximization isn't an argument against money. The argument against financial maximization is that while it makes some people much richer, it can also create financial *in*stability for many more people at the same time.

The case against financial maximization isn't anti-money. It's pro-money. It's just pro-people, too. In service of people, money can be a very positive force. But when we live our lives serving money—by choice or because we have no choice—we severely limit our potential.

THE IMPORTANCE OF MONEY

In 1943, a thirty-five-year-old sociologist named Abraham Maslow published a paper in *Psychological Review* called "A Theory of Human Motivation."

In it, Maslow presented a theory that people move through a series of needs in their lives, and that each need is a stepping-stone to the next. Maslow saw five needs that people move through:

1. Physiological needs (food, water, shelter)
2. Safety (health, physical, financial)
3. Love (family, friendships, belonging)
4. Esteem (the drive to achieve, live meaningfully, be recognized)
5. Self-actualization ("to become everything that one is capable of becoming")

Ideally, a person's life progresses through these stages. After they've satisfied their survival need, they'd focus on safety. Once they've satisfied their needs for survival and safety, they'd focus on love or esteem. And so on.

If one of these needs isn't met, however, a person would be unable to move further. They wouldn't even see the next step. Here's how Maslow explained it:

"If all the needs are unsatisfied, and the organism is then dominated by the physiological needs, all other needs may become simply non-existent or be pushed into the background. It is then fair to characterize the whole organism by saying simply that it is hungry, for consciousness is almost completely preempted by hunger ... The urge to write poetry, the desire to acquire an automobile, the interest in American history, the desire for a new pair of shoes are, in the extreme case, forgotten or become of secondary importance."

This is how the first two need levels—survival and safety—function. If a person feels unsafe, pursuing love or esteem are very difficult, and in some cases impossible. If a person is sick or has significant financial problems (in America, those two tragically often go together), life is primarily about getting well and out of the red.

Once a need is satisfied, it vanishes into the background. According to Maslow, a satisfied need exists like "a filled bottle has emptiness." The previous hunger is forgotten but can return.

This concept is commonly referred to as "Maslow's hierarchy of needs." It remains one of the most widely cited frameworks for understanding human behavior. A common visualization of the hierarchy (not made by Maslow) presents the five needs as a pyramid, where each need provides the foundation for the one above. But as Maslow points out, the order is "not nearly as rigid" as people think.

In Maslow's original paper, money is never mentioned as one of the needs. The 1940s were very different from today. But in the modern world, the need for financial security is as fundamental as the need for physical safety. This means money is very important.

But in Maslow's hierarchy, money is also quite "low" on the list. Though some people use money as a proxy for self-esteem, money is not a higher value on its own. It is, however, a necessary foundation for the pursuit of higher values.

A 2010 study by the Nobel Prize–winning behavioral economist Daniel Kahneman sheds interesting light on this idea. Kahneman found a "statistically significant and quantitatively important" correlation between emotional well-being and income. The more money someone made, his research discovered, the happier the person was.

But this was true only up to a point. The research found that up until a salary of $75,000 this was the case. But once someone made more than that, the impact of more money on their emotional well-being was much smaller. Happiness didn't keep going up with a person's salary at the same rate. Surprisingly, this means that a list of ten random people who make at least $75,000 a year could be just as happy as the ten richest people in the world. Maybe even happier.

This $75,000 threshold seems odd until you consider it from Maslow's perspective.

As people make more money, they fulfill their need for financial security. As they become more secure, their well-being grows. And it turns out that there may be an actual point where they satisfy their need for financial safety. Kahneman's research suggests that, in America, around $75,000 a year might be that point.

But why doesn't emotional well-being keep increasing the same way as people make more money?

Because the more you have of something, the less more of it means to you. Once a person has satisfied his or her financial security, being "more financially secure" doesn't make as meaningful a difference. Economists call this phenomenon "diminishing returns." Like drinking more water after you've already quenched your thirst.

Think about the other two safety needs in that tier: your health and your safety from physical harm. Societies fulfill these needs for citizens in egalitarian ways. They provide for physical safety through laws and police, and for the health of their citizens through nationalized health care (in all developed countries except the United States). Unlike money, both are made equally available to all.

But if physical safety were distributed like wealth is today at our current levels of inequality, Jeff Bezos would have a personal police force of 845 cops while 163 million Americans would share 1,565 police officers between them. That's one for every 104,000 people. At that ratio, all of New York City would have a total police force of just 82 cops wearing NYPD blue.

This is obviously absurd. Jeff Bezos's 837th cop wouldn't be making him any safer. They'd just be getting Bezos's 836th cop his or her coffee. Those officers would mean much more in a neighborhood that needs them. Just like Bezos's 135 billionth dollar means less to him than it would to someone who lacks financial security.

This isn't to say that Bezos's 135 billionth dollar is unethical or unearned. This money did not just magically and luckily appear in his possession. It's to note that as someone has more money, it has less meaning for that person. In a universe of financial maximization, this is its own kind of trap.

. . . .

While writing this book I gave a talk to a couple hundred CEOs at an event in upstate New York. Along with the Kickstarter story, I presented the case that financial maximization was hurting us.

I could see by their faces that some in the audience really connected with this message. And I could see that many others did not. Afterward I spent over an hour talking to people in each group.

The conversation I remember most was with the CEO of a midsized construction business. He walked up with a visor on his head, a cigar sticking out of the side of his mouth, and a twinkle in his eye. I had no idea what to expect.

"It's funny," he told me. "Before I made money, I was a die-hard capitalist. But now that I've made money, I don't know what I am."

I listened as he told me his story. He'd learned that money wasn't as meaningful as he thought, but he still felt the drive to make an impact on the world. He didn't have a clue what that meant he should do.

Maslow would know what to tell the construction CEO: that he was at the precipice of his next step. The next levels—love, esteem, self-actualization, and beyond—were calling to him.

This is a step many people struggle with. You go to school to learn how to become very well off financially. Nobody asks what's supposed to happen after that.

This is where all of society is currently stuck. By focusing on financial maximization we're treating the second rung of Maslow's hierarchy like it's the summit. But to become everything that we're capable of becoming, we have to keep climbing. How can our goal be anything short of that?

WHAT DRIVES THE DRIVEN

We take it on faith that by maximizing money, all else will follow. Because money can be exchanged for other things, the growth of money grows everything else.

Under certain conditions, this could be true. If the goal were to grow the economy so that every citizen could attain financial security, money could very well lead to the growth of everything else.

But financial maximization isn't about broad financial security. Financial maximization doesn't believe in financial security. Financial maximization is about growing your own pile. And when it comes to pile-growing, there's no such thing as enough.

As Maslow's hierarchy of needs makes clear, when the accrual of wealth becomes the point of life, we limit ourselves. Money makes the world go around, but only at a fraction of its potential. It isn't the highest we can go. As long as financial maximization is our focus, the biggest payoffs will remain disappointingly out of reach.

The dogma of rational self-interest has convinced us that maximizing our immediate desires is the only rational strategy.

It's the empirically correct thing to do. But there's plenty of evidence that this is not the case.

In the book *Drive*, the sociologist Daniel Pink writes about a study at Carnegie Mellon in 1969. In the study researchers gave each participant a stack of blocks to use to make shapes. Participants were given a set time to make as many different shapes as they could.

The participant was focused on making shapes, but this was not the experiment's focus. The real experiment began midway through the test when the researcher left the room during a break. Through a two-way mirror, the researchers tracked how long each participant played with the blocks while on their own, rather than doing the 1969 version of looking at their phone, like picking up a magazine. During the break most participants continued to play with the blocks.

The next day the experiment was repeated, with one difference. This time some of the participants were told they'd be paid a dollar for each shape they made. For the other participants, there was no mention of payment.

Once again, the researchers left the room for a break. And again, the researchers tracked how long each participant played with the blocks while they were gone. They saw a difference. Participants who were promised money spent more time playing with the blocks during the break than those who were not.

The third and final day, the participants came back again. This time the group that had previously been paid were told there wasn't enough money to pay them that day. The third session would be unpaid like the first one. The unpaid group continued to be unpaid.

Midway through the test the researchers again left the room to see what the participants did. And here again, they saw a difference.

The people who'd been paid the day before spent much less time playing the game during the break. Less time than the day they were paid and less time than the first day, too.

We can sympathize with the paid and then unpaid participants. You're not paying me for something you paid me for yesterday? What a rip-off! We'd probably have the same reaction. But arguably there's an even deeper injustice going on.

Consider the behavior of the group that was never paid. On the third day, they played the game longer than ever. They enjoyed it and wanted to play more. They were having fun.

Before the researchers offered money, the other group felt the same way. But once money entered and exited the picture, this changed. The game was no longer fun. It was about money.

The paid participants had a few more dollars than the unpaid participants. That's something. But they lost something, too: a joy that the other group got to experience.

Pink references more than one hundred studies that reveal similar results. In many situations, money can be a demotivating force. Everything from performance in a game to rates of giving blood to deciding whether to allow nuclear power in your town. In each of these cases researchers found that people were more effective or more generous when money was not involved. Once money entered the picture, people didn't perform as well. They became guarded. They didn't want to lose.

Money as the basis of life and society sets a ceiling on what we can be. It doesn't inspire our best selves. It doesn't aim for the peak of the pyramid.

Pink names three drives that he believes speak to our higher values. Pink identifies:

1. Autonomy: the desire to have a say over what we do
2. Mastery: the process of getting better at what we do
3. Purpose: the meaning behind what we do

When we're pursuing these kinds of goals, Pink suggests, we're at our best. These drives are not far from the highest tiers on Maslow's hierarchy.

The implications of what Maslow and Pink suggest are far-reaching. They also directly contradict the ethos of financial maximization.

They imply there's a proper place for money and an improper place for money. They provide evidence that there are important values distinct from financial value. And they strongly suggest that basing our choices on nonfinancial values is rational and advantageous. If we pursue values higher than money, they suggest, our potential will grow.

HOW WE TRACK VALUE TODAY

For the past hundred years we've measured value through a metric called gross domestic product (GDP). GDP tracks how much money businesses, consumers, and the government spend each quarter in a given country. (This is a simplification of how GDP is calculated; you can Google the actual formula if you're curious.)

When GDP goes up, businesses, consumers, and government are spending more money than in the recent past. In economic terms, this is referred to as a growing economy. When GDP goes down, this means less money is being spent. When this happens for at least six months, this is called a recession.

The person who introduced GDP to the world was an economist named Simon Kuznets. Kuznets proposed GDP after the Great Depression as a bird's-eye view of what was happening in the economy. Within a decade it became a global standard. Today virtually all economies on Earth are measured this same way.

When Kuznets proposed the metric, he pointed out some of its limitations. In the original proposal to Congress in 1934, he warned:

"No income measurement undertakes to estimate the reverse side of income, that is, the intensity and unpleasantness of effort going into the earning of income. The welfare of a nation can, therefore, scarcely be inferred from a measurement of national income as defined above."

Since some people are forced to sacrifice their personal safety or values ("the intensity and unpleasantness of effort") to earn their paychecks, Kuznets said, we cannot conclude that their income and well-being are the same thing.

The same problem exists on the other side of the ledger, too.

GDP tracks how much money is spent but not how or why it's spent. GDP sees spending $1,000 on a family vacation and $1,000 on a divorce attorney as the same. Both are a thousand dollars of GDP. It's about how much, not why.

According to GDP, then, the ideal citizen would drive an SUV, have cancer (chemotherapy can be very GDP-positive), be getting a divorce, and eat out every night. According to our predominant measurement of value, this would be ideal. If we all lived this way, GDP would skyrocket.

We recognize that this isn't right, of course. But when there's such a disparity between what the measurement system says is good and what our experience tells us is good, we have a problem. At the heart of this problem is the relationship between two very similar words.

VALUE AND VALUES

Though the words "value" and "values" appear basically identical, we tend to think of them as distinct concepts.

If you ask someone about their values, you're likely to get their best articulation of the ideals that are important to them. The things they believe in and that define them.

If you ask someone what the value of something is, that person will think a few seconds before providing an approximate sense of value: answers like "a lot," "not much," a number, or a comparison to something else.

We think of "value" (singular) as what something is worth. We think of "values" (plural) as what's worth something to somebody.

Value means money. Value is an economics word.

Values means ideals. Values is a humanities word.

Value is a form of measurement. Values are a form of categorization. One is quantitative and the other is qualitative. Both relate to the goodness or importance of things.

We're surrounded by measurements of economic value. Prices, stocks, financial measurements like GDP.

We're surrounded by idealistic values, too, but in less visible ways.

Values are an ancient and powerful operating system. We don't really understand how they work. We even struggle to articulate what our values are. But we can feel their influence.

Values form who we aspire to be. Values ground us in what we most care about. Values are what the angel on our shoulder says we ought to do. Values are why the right choices for us are what they are.

But as the supernatural tenor of these descriptions suggests, values aren't easy to identify. They're even harder to measure.

This is the problem that the economic perspective of value alleviates. Unlike inner dialogues and philosophical monologues about values, value in the form of a price is something anyone can understand. Money is a globally relevant language. This is enormously convenient.

As the force of financial maximization grew, society shifted from a focus on values (what's right and wrong, what's meaningful) to a focus on value (maximizing, optimizing). Our choices stopped being about ideals and became about money.

There are understandable reasons for this. Value can be more precise than values. Value is easier to compare across contexts. There are many technological tools for measuring value (singular) and few for values (plural). The measured surpassed the not-measured.

But when our only concept of value is financial, there's cognitive dissonance between how people want to live and how our metrics want us to live. This is a dangerous misalignment.

Remember, our main value metric (GDP) counts something as valuable only if money is spent on it. According to this logic, the only value that Google and Twitter add to the world are the ad units they sell. The dissemination of knowledge is not valuable, but data harvesting and targeted advertising are valuable. What we see as the fatal drawback of these services is what our current concept of value sees as their whole point.

GDP sees the domestic work of women and men in their own homes (estimated at $12 trillion in unaccounted-for GDP for women alone) as not valuable, while a woman or man cleaning another person's house is valuable.

GDP sees Wikipedia as possibly having a negative value. If there wasn't Wikipedia people would still buy encyclopedias. And all those volunteer Wikipedia editors could do something really valuable with their time, like work for money.

My point isn't just to criticize GDP. Every metric can be made to look silly if pushed beyond its natural boundaries.

My point is that the reality of value is already beyond our measurement systems. Our answer to this shouldn't be to ignore what's beyond our sensors. It should be to learn more about the values that exist outside of our current understanding. Financial value is a key value for sure, but we know that it's not the only one.

Where we've ended up isn't surprising. We invest enormously in optimization. We "measure what matters." Therefore, if we don't measure it or can't measure it, it must not matter. And values are not something we know how to consistently measure right now.

The way we think about value keeps us low on Maslow's hierarchy. When we aim low, what higher values are we losing sight of? To find those, we'll need a different way to see.

CHAPTER SEVEN

BENTOISM

EXPANDING THE UNIVERSE

When I picture the self-interest that dominates the world today, I imagine a simple graph. On the x-axis is time. On the y-axis is some value—money, power, units sold—that's exponentially growing.

In business and tech this is called a "hockey stick" graph. A chart where whatever is being measured is growing so fast, the line goes up and to the right. This is the ultimate best-case outcome for any decision.

But this idea of "making it" is just a sliver of what's out there. While we so intently focus on maximizing our self-interest, there's a larger universe that we miss. When we take a step back, this bigger picture starts to emerge.

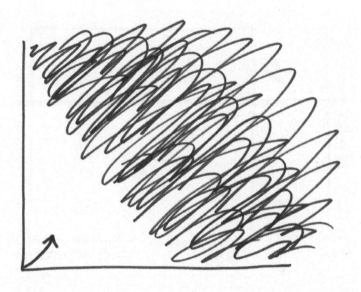

Our self-interest doesn't stop with us right now. We don't exist in a vacuum. We live within communities of people who are affected by our decisions, and whose decisions affect us. Our decisions impact our future selves, too.

We can see it on our graph. The x-axis of Time extends from now all the way into the future. And the y-axis of Self-Interest extends from you ("Me") to your family, friends, and communities ("Us").

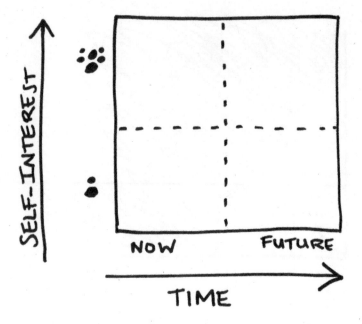

In this expanded view of self-interest, what we want right now is still there. But so are other rational perspectives. There's our future self to think about. The people we care about. And the future of our children and everybody else's children, too.

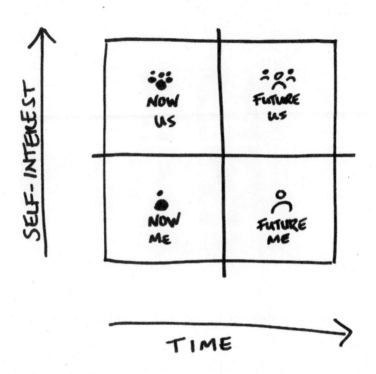

Each of these spaces impacts us and is impacted by us. Their perspectives are in our rational self-interest.

I call this way of seeing Bentoism. "Bento" as in a bento box, the Japanese packed meal.

"Bento" comes from a Japanese word meaning convenience. A bento box is always filled with a variety of dishes. Not too much of any one thing. The bento honors the Japanese philosophy of *hara hachi bu*, which says the goal of a meal is to be 80 percent full. The bento box creates a convenient and healthy hidden default.

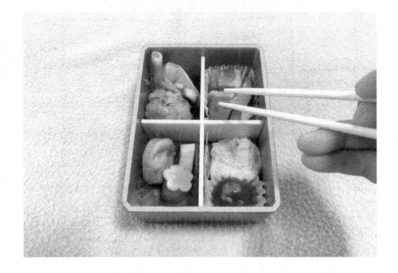

Bentoism is a bento box for our values and decisions. A more balanced view of what's in our rational self-interest. A way to rediscover the values that today we find hard to see.

THE PRISONER'S BENTO

Earlier I described the Prisoner's Dilemma, a game where two players in separate interrogation rooms must choose whether to be loyal to each other and go to jail or inform on each other and go free. Because of the parameters of the game, informing on your partner is the rational thing to do.

You may recall that when the secretaries at RAND played the game, they didn't inform on each other. They stuck together and achieved the game's best outcome of less time served overall. But according to the logic of the game, they didn't play rationally. The rational move was to maximize your own self-interest, which meant betraying your partner rather than staying loyal to him or her.

What does a Bentoist perspective make of Prisoner's Dilemma?

To find out, we ask each Bento box the question: Should we stay loyal to our partner or should we inform on our partner? How do the perspectives in each Bento respond?

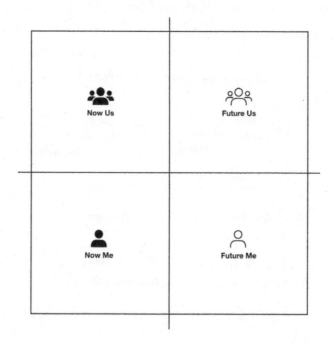

Now Me is the most self-interested voice. It's in self-preservation mode. It's ready to tell the authorities anything to avoid jail.

Now Us considers the people around us, their needs, and how our choices affect them. Its instincts are for solidarity. It doesn't want to send our partner to jail.

Future Me is the person you want to be. It doesn't want you to make a decision you'll later regret. It reminds you of your values (whatever those are) and encourages you to stay true to them.

Future Us is the world you want your children to have. How things ought to be. Future Us would rather live in a world where people can trust each other than one where they can't.

The debate is between the voices of Now Me and Now Us. But the decision is made by the values of Future Me. It's a person's values that ultimately make the call.

Should I stay quiet or confess?

You should never betray a friend **Now Us** QUIET	The world needs more loyalty **Future Us** QUIET
I don't want to go to jail **Now Me** CONFESS	My relationships are everything! **Future Me** QUIET

The RAND secretaries chose Now Us over Now Me because that's what their values told them to do. According to the logic of

the game this was irrational because they weren't maximizing their self-interest. But according to Bentoism, they were acting on their rational self-interest, just a broader idea of it than Prisoner's Dilemma accommodates.

Prisoner's Dilemma shows the rationality of maximizing one's self-interest—and underlines how limited our view of self-interest is at the same time. When we can't see beyond Now Me, the world looks like a battle between self-interested individuals. The dominance of financial maximization depends on this limited perspective. When our idea of what's in our rational self-interest is limited, our idea of value is, too.

EXPANDING VALUE

Bentoism isn't a utopian clean slate. It builds on the world around us.

Like financial maximization, Bentoism strives for rational and measurable principles. Bentoism seeks to expand some of the tools of financial maximization to a wider set of values. And like Adam Smith, Bentoism believes good things happen when people act in their rational self-interest.

But Bentoism also believes that our definitions of "rational" and "self-interest" are too narrow. We think rational value means financial value. And self-interest is all about satisfying our immediate desires. But neither perspective comes close to the full spectrum of what's valuable or rational.

Today's thinking goes:

1. It's rational to behave in your self-interest.

2. Maximization of financial value is in your self-interest.

3. Therefore, financial maximization is the rational value all the time.

Bentoism goes:

1. It's rational to behave in your self-interest.

2. Your values and context shape your self-interest.

3. Therefore, making values- and context-specific decisions is rational all the time.

Aristotle said value resides in "the proper activity or functioning of things according to their nature." The goal of Bentoism is to help us find the proper values and ways of valuing in all that we do. As simple as this sounds, this is the critical shift that can move us past the dominance of financial maximization.

Financial maximization imposes a monotheistic perspective on value. Only money and its henchmen, like envy and greed, are free to operate according to their nature. All other values must operate according to money's demands. Science is valued so long as it produces profits. Creativity is valued if it works at the box office. Generosity is valued when it lifts brand awareness.

But value is not monotheistic. Value is pluralistic. Different people and communities rightly aspire to and follow different ideals. And different contexts rationally call on different values.

If you're trying to decide between investing in Company A or Company B, asking which will produce the bigger financial return is a rational and appropriate way to make a decision. Asking which company is more courageous or more beautiful is less likely to lead to the ideal outcome. They're not the most relevant values to consult.

When a judge decides which party in a legal dispute should prevail, the values of justice and the law are rational and appropriate. Not which side is more attractive, has more influence, or spent more money on their argument.

That's the idea anyway. But financial maximization is a dominating force. Values and philosophies that should rightly govern our thinking don't because of the dominance of financial maximization. Financial maximization justly dominates some domains, but many others it dominates tyrannically. The bulldozing of community values by financial values in the Lower East Side, for instance.

While financial maximization demands we focus on the here and now, other values think bigger. Love encourages us to let go of our selfishness to be a better partner. Grit pushes us to keep trying even when we want to give up. Courage inspires us to step up on a dangerous mission. These values rightly demand we sacrifice our immediate self-interest for a bigger payoff.

These are decisions that today's rationally self-interested mind-set gets wrong. Except in specific circumstances, the focus on financial value misses the values and ways of valuing that will lead to the best outcomes. Its view of value is too limited. In those situations, values other than financial value should be our guide.

THE GOLD WATCH

In the movie *Pulp Fiction*, Bruce Willis plays a boxer named Butch.

Butch is an aging fighter with one last fight in him. And he agrees to throw that fight after being paid off by a gangster. "In the fifth [round] my ass goes down," Butch dutifully repeats for him.

But when the time comes, Butch doesn't do it. He wins the fight, double-crosses the mob, and jumps out a window. Safe in a motel room with his lover, Fabienne, Butch is ready to go on the run.

Except.

Except that when preparing for their escape, Butch discovers that Fabienne forgot to pack his watch. And not just any watch. His war hero father's gold watch. The same gold watch that Christopher Walken's character memorably describes hiding in an uncomfortable place earlier in the movie.

Though the gangsters are almost certainly waiting for him, Butch decides to go back to his apartment to get it. From there Butch experiences, as he later says, "without a doubt the single weirdest day of my life." Which is putting it mildly. He has several near-death encounters and multiple people are killed. All because he went back for a watch.

So was Butch's choice to go back rational?

This seems like an odd question. But remember, the hidden

default of the modern world is that maximizing the here and now is the only rational way to behave. Is that what Butch is doing? Is he maximizing his self-interest?

It doesn't seem like it. If he was acting in his rational self-interest, wouldn't he just buy another watch? And yet Butch, a character that seems rational enough, chooses to go back.

Before disregarding Butch's choice as the kind of crazy thing that only happens in movies, we should consider whether a perspective exists that would make the choice rational. Try to see it through his eyes. Is there some value he sees that we don't?

In Quentin Tarantino's original *Pulp Fiction* script, there's a scene that didn't make the final cut that helps answer this question. In it, Butch is driving back to get the watch when he starts second-guessing his decision. He pulls over, gets out of the car, and starts talking to himself.

BUTCH

I ain't gonna do this. This is a punchy move and I ain't punchy! Daddy would totally fuckin' understand. If he was here right now, he'd say, "Butch, git a grip. It's a fuckin' watch, man. You lose one, ya git another. This is your life you're fuckin' around with, which you shouldn't be doin', 'cause you only got one."

Butch continues to pace, but now he's silent. Then . . .

BUTCH

This is my war. You see, Butch, what you're forgettin' is this watch isn't just a device that enables you to keep track of time. This watch is a symbol. It's a symbol of how your father, and his father before him, and his father before him, distinguished themselves in war. And when I took Marsellus Wallace's money, I started a war. This is my World War Two. That apartment in North Hollywood, that's my Wake Island. In fact, if you look at it that way, it's almost kismet that Fabienne left it behind. And using that perspective, going back for it isn't stupid. It may be dangerous, but it's not stupid. Because there are certain things in this world that are worth going back for.

In Butch's monologue we can hear his decision-making process. It almost sounds like he's checking a Bento.

Now Me says leave. It's just a watch. "I ain't gonna do this. This is a punchy move and I ain't punchy!"

Now Us says think of Fabienne—and leave. "This is your life you're fuckin' around with."

Future Me reminds Butch of his values and encourages him to stay true. "What you're forgettin' is this watch isn't just a device that enables you to keep track of time. This watch is a symbol."

Future Us tells Butch that the watch symbolizes his family legacy. He *has* to go back and get it. "It's almost kismet that Fabienne left it behind."

Should I go back for the watch?

Think of Fabienne — it's just a watch **Now Us** NO	The Butch family never backs down from a fight **Future Us** YES
It's not worth dying for — LEAVE! **Now Me** NO	The watch is a symbol of my heritage **Future Me** YES

Seen through the lens of Bentoism, Butch's decision is rational. As he says, "It may be dangerous, but it's not stupid. Because there are certain things in this world that are worth going back for." Things like values. By choosing rationally using a Bento-like perspective, Butch finds his values, gets the watch, and lives to see another day.

BENTO VALUES

In a complicated world, financial maximization is a simplifier. It's a hammer that turns all of life into a nail. There's just one goal: to make as much money as possible. The rest will take care of itself.

Butch's Bento-like process, on the other hand, seems like *work*. He self-examines. He adjusts. At first blush, this may seem arduous and even inconvenient. Another thing we have to start thinking about?

That's probably how some people felt when the screwdriver was invented in the late fifteenth century. Up until then, every problem really was a nail waiting to be hammered. So why are we suddenly complicating matters with another thing? Hammers built Noah's Ark, didn't they? Was that not good enough?

People back then didn't know it, but hammer-only life was limited. The screwdriver opened up new possibilities. Construction became more intricate. Materials became lighter. New fields of engineering were created. All because of a new tool.

Bentoism is also a tool: a values processor. "What does my Bento say?" is a metaphysical "Phillips or flathead?" A self-check for what fits the matter at hand.

Each Bento has its own core values and ways of valuing that set the norms for that space. They don't encompass every value possibility. Just what's at the root level.

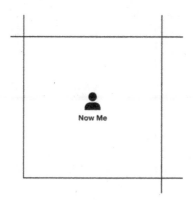

Now Me is about the here and now. This is life as we know it today. In Now Me the governing values are security, pleasure, and autonomy.

Security reflects the first rungs of Abraham Maslow's hierarchy of needs. Security is the voice that pushes us to provide for ourselves. The drive for money that's actually in our best interest. This value governs Now Me because Now Me's job is to keep us safe from harm.

Pleasure is a wild card. Pleasure can be a wonderfully valid reason to do something. To pursue and experience pleasure is to be human. But pleasure can easily lead us astray. Most activity today is in pursuit of either security or pleasure.

Autonomy is having the freedom to decide what we will and will not do. Autonomy exists in both immature states (not listening to sound advice) and mature states (finding the thing we're best at and doing it in the way that's best for us). For some, the pursuit of autonomy is the ultimate goal. For others it's terrifying. Someone who strongly desires security, for example, may willingly give up their autonomy to get it.

Now Us is a space for our relationships and interactions with others. In Now Us the governing values are community, fairness, and tradition.

Community, as in our families and others who we rely on and who rely on us. What do they need from us and what do we need from them? Who fits into this box changes based on the context: family, friends, coworkers, neighbors, people who share the same faith, even people playing together in co-op mode.

Fairness expands our consideration not just to encompass those we directly care about, but to imagine ourselves in the shoes of others. It asks that people be treated the way that we would like to be treated. Fairness demands justice, and just justice at that. Fairness is critical for another reason. In a future where financial value is merely the market leader of value rather than its monopolist, the principles of fairness would guide values conflicts as they came up.

Tradition creates and reinforces Us-ness by celebrating shared experiences and rituals. We greatly underestimate the power and benefits of tradition. Tradition increases the richness of life by creating parallel experiences with the past and—by continuation of the tradition—the future. ("You slept in this bed as a baby and now your daughter will, too." "It's almost kismet that Fabienne left [the watch] behind.")

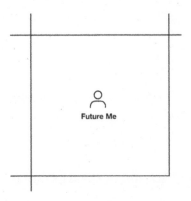

Future Me is about our legacy and personal values. In Future Me the governing values are mastery, purpose, and grit.

Mastery is passionate about the process of getting better, no matter how good one already is. The pursuit of mastery is what makes Jiro dream of sushi and every Beatles album better than the one before. Growth in the pursuit of mastery is the purest of goals. Mastery doesn't demand more resources of the Earth or anyone else. It demands more of us.

Purpose gives our choices clarity and meaning. Purpose sharpens our talents and harnesses them for a worthy cause. Purpose makes the mundane or the seemingly distasteful meaningful. Purpose can be a religion, a cause, or a goal.

Grit expresses itself as a kind of stick-to-it-iveness. Grit encourages us to stay true to our values and convictions. To live the life of the obituary we wish to have.

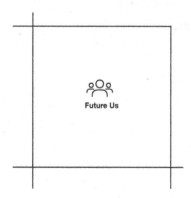

Future Us

Finally, Future Us is about the world that future generations will experience. In Future Us, the governing values are awareness, sustainability, and knowledge.

Awareness asks us to think through the implications. Have we imagined what would happen if everyone made this choice? Are we playing out the long-term effects? We struggle at anticipating the future for good reason: the world changes in ways that we cannot predict. But many of those changes we can predict with careful study. A peaceful existence relies on disasters prevented.

Sustainability encourages us to make decisions that can be permanent. Today we believe we "can't afford" many of the sustainable solutions we will one day have to implement because of climate change. This has it backward. We can afford to sacrifice today for the future. What we can't afford is the other way around.

Knowledge increases our capacity for awareness, sustainability, and all other forms of value. The accrual and application of knowledge is a force multiplier that can spark everything from technology to science to philosophy, and new ways of life with them. Gains through knowledge raise the floor for all of society. Yet new knowledge is often feared and despised because it challenges the ruling order. It was eating from the Tree of Knowledge that got Adam and Eve expelled from Eden, after all.

Here are the Bentos and their governing values all together:

Governing Values

Now Us

Community
Fairness
Tradition

Future Us

Awareness
Sustainability
Knowledge

Now Me

Security
Pleasure
Autonomy

Future Me

Mastery
Purpose
Grit

Bentoism expands our perspective beyond Now Me, and challenges the assumption that financial value is the only rational value to consider. All of these values are rational reasons to act. They're valid reasons why something should or should not happen. What's rationally valuable and in our rational self-interest is bigger than we think.

An expansion of understanding along these lines isn't unprecedented. Just go to the doctor to experience it for yourself.

HOW HEALTH BECAME HEALTHY

On a hot Saturday morning in July 1881, the recently inaugurated president James Garfield walked into a train station in Washington, DC.

As Garfield prepared to board his train, a man stepped out of the crowd, pulled out a pistol, and shot Garfield in the back. "My God, what is this?" Garfield exclaimed. The man shot again. Garfield fell to the ground, still conscious.

The bullets had missed Garfield's organs and spine, but one was still inside of him. The doctors desperately wanted it out. The president was given champagne and morphine while fifteen different doctors searched the wound with their fingers and instruments. They couldn't find it.

Garfield survived the night, but the repeated excavations for the bullet created a bigger problem. No sterilization of any kind was used.

Garfield suffered in agony as infection seized his body. Dirty fingers prodded his open, pus-infected wounds in swampy heat. He was afflicted with blood poisoning and pneumonia. His weight dropped from 200 pounds to 135. After seventy-nine days of misery, he died.

Later, during the trial of Garfield's shooter, the assassin claimed, "The doctors killed Garfield, I just shot him." He was found guilty and hung not long after.

From today's vantage, the assassin's claim is not without merit. If Garfield's wounds happened today, he would have gone home in a couple of days. Instead, he died.

Not that long ago, even the president's doctors had what we would consider a rudimentary understanding of health. In 1881, germs were still a novel idea. The antiseptic method, which taught doctors to sterilize hands, instruments, and wounds, was growing in use in Europe, where surgeon Joseph Lister invented it in 1865, but wasn't yet widely practiced in the United States. One of the president's dozen doctors had even attended a lecture given by Lister about it. Unfortunately for Garfield, the doctor had not been persuaded.

The president's doctors weren't alone in their ineptitude. For more than 2,000 years many doctors were more likely to make a patient worse than better. For most of human history, the practice of medicine was a routinely terrible thing.

But in the nineteenth century, the myth of the curing effects of medicine miraculously began to become real. New discoveries made previously false promises a reality.

A VERY BRIEF HISTORY OF HEALTH

The first great innovations in health came a long time ago. Like, 400 BCE long ago. Hippocrates, the so-called father of medicine, became the first doctor to establish that health and illness were caused by natural factors (diet, environment, living habits), not as a form of punishment by the gods. Until this point, belief that illness was supernaturally derived was common. Men and women watched their health by doing as the gods wished.

Hippocrates and his followers changed this view by striving for a more empirical perspective. They carefully cataloged case records and symptoms to diagnose diseases. Many of their discoveries and ideas remain relevant today.

Still, this was 400 BCE. Their understanding of what was in our bodies, how they functioned, and the source of illness was all wrong. Hippocrates believed in the "four humors." This theory suggested that the body's health was regulated by four fluids: blood, phlegm, yellow bile, and black bile (which does not actually exist). Sickness was caused by their lack of balance.

This was standard belief among physicians for the next 2,200 years. You read that right: more than 2,000 years. Someone seeing a doctor in 1800 may have gotten the same medical care as a contemporary of Jesus. Considering that no tools existed to see inside the human body while it was alive and that burial customs limited opportunities to autopsy the dead, this was understandable. Doctors were flying blind.

During those 2,200 years, most illnesses were treated by one of three methods: purging (inducing vomiting or diarrhea), cautery (putting a hot iron on the skin), or, most commonly, bloodletting. Bloodletting meant cutting into an artery (or, if you were fashionable, using leeches) and intentionally bleeding the patient, preferably until he or she passed out. This was thought to bring the body's fluids into balance.

Bleeding was the "take a Tylenol" of its day. And that day lasted for more than 2,000 years.

But in the middle of the nineteenth century, this began to change.

Three events stand out as catalysts. In Budapest, a doctor named Ignaz Semmelweis identified microbes on doctors' dirty hands as the cause of a deadly form of childbirth fever. In Paris, a scientist named Louis Pasteur proved that germs existed, establishing a new idea called germ theory and discovering the actual microbes that Semmelweis theorized were the cause of illness. And in Glasgow, a doctor named Joseph Lister created the antiseptic method by applying the principles of germ theory to surgical care. Before Lister's innovation, more than 80 percent of patients died from postsurgical infections.

After these discoveries, doctors and scientists could finally see what was happening beneath the surface of the human body. And through trial and error, they learned how to manipulate these microscopic elements to directly and positively affect human health for the first time.

But as the death of President Garfield sixteen years later shows, these ideas were not immediately accepted. When Semmelweis found the cause of childbirth fever, there was no celebration. There was resistance. Acknowledging the ineffectiveness of medical care would also mean acknowledging the culpability of physicians in the deaths of past patients. This was not an easy thing to confront.

But the flood of new knowledge eventually made its way into common practice. The discovery of germs and microbes inspired huge changes in public health and sanitation. Infant mortality decreased 90 percent, maternal mortality decreased 99 percent, and life expectancy almost doubled in the twentieth century. Half of the medicines commonly in use by 1950 were completely unknown just a decade before. Because of extended life expectancy and the growth of medicine, more grandparents have a relationship with their grandchildren today than ever before. The world changed.

Medicine went from a "fantasy of a science," as historian David Wootton puts it, into an actual science. How did it happen? There were three driving forces, ones that are often present in times of great progress.

First is **technology**, and not just medical technology. The transformation of health began with the invention of the printing press, which allowed physicians to easily compare techniques and outcomes. The printing press was followed by a long line of technologies, including the microscope, the stethoscope, the data table (for sharing experiment results), anesthesia, the computer, and other tools to help us better observe and influence the body's processes.

Next is **measurement**. Measurement was transformational

even in its simplest forms. Ignaz Semmelweis discovered the cause of childbirth fever by counting the death rates of two maternity wards. The doctor John Snow helped stop a deadly cholera outbreak in London by counting where deaths occurred and finding a water pump that was infecting the population. Counting mortality rates led to the conclusion that bloodletting was harmful after 2,200 years of practice. Measurement removed the guesswork. It definitively revealed what worked and what didn't.

Last is **specificity**. Aided by technology and measurement, the body came to be understood as a system of distinct parts. Everything was connected but not everything worked the same way. Each part of the body had its own path to health. It wasn't one treatment fits all. Now we know there are types and stages of cancer, good and bad cholesterols, good and bad fats, and more nuance every day. (Specificity is the same force that Adam Smith declares crucial to unlocking economic growth in *The Wealth of Nations*.)

Because of the forces of technology, measurement, and specificity, our understanding of health became deeper. Medicine became real. We live longer and better lives as a result.

The same thing can happen again.

Financial maximization is to value what bloodletting was to medicine: the most advanced answer of its time, but not the final answer. Value-wise, we're still in the Dark Ages. We've barely scratched the surface. We don't yet know what we don't yet know.

Bentoism is like a rudimentary microscope for value. A way of going from 1x to 4x the magnification. With a broader view, the same forces that deepened our understanding of health can deepen our understanding of value. Our ability to create value can significantly expand as a result.

THE GOLD WATCH (CONTINUED)

The value judgments made by the secretaries at the RAND Corporation and Butch in *Pulp Fiction* may not seem like much, but they're not easy computations. Butch and the secretaries had to apply the lessons of the past to the present, look for deeper causes, and compare very different kinds of values.

This is more than what the typical algorithm can do. Algorithms learn by running millions of consequence-free simulations to find which option is most likely to produce the ideal outcome. It's discovery by brute force, like Edison's thousands of experiments before finding the right mixture of materials to make the filament for the lightbulb.

We humans don't get to run a million iterations. We only get to live life once. We need every tool we can find to make the best decisions.

This is why a broader spectrum of values is so crucial. Values are a guidance system based on the collective wisdom of our ancestors and the inputs of our cultures. Values are what make right and wrong. We ignore them at our peril.

Bentoism rationally expands the field of vision to a wider spectrum of values. It builds a muscle memory into our thinking that allows us to access these important but harder-to-reach spaces. The spaces where better choices and more impactful values await.

Expanding the value spectrum isn't an irrational choice. The irrational choice is to keep ignoring it. As some people are already learning, expanding the idea of value isn't just a rational next step. It's a competitive advantage.

ADELE GOES ON TOUR

THE SINGER-SONGWRITER ADELE IS ONE OF THE BIGGEST pop stars in the world. She's won fifteen Grammys, taken home an Oscar, and sold more than 60 million copies of her albums *19*, *21*, and *25*—each named for her age when she made it.

Adele achieved this while being an independently minded artist. Born and raised in South London, Adele does not come from privilege. Her mother had her when she was young and her father left when she was two. When Adele was discovered as a teenager, it was by a small, influential indie label through a Myspace demo.

Adele carries this background proudly as a pop star. As she told a Norwegian interviewer in 2015, "I don't know how I'm meant to make records for people to relate to and enjoy if I'm living some mad life."

People do relate to Adele—in record numbers. But her

overwhelming popularity creates a problem. When tickets for her concerts go on sale, they instantly sell out. Originally bought at a face value of around $50 (well below what artists at her level tend to charge), her tickets immediately appear on secondary ticketing websites for hundreds and even thousands of dollars more.

How does this happen? Does Adele have especially entrepreneurial fans? Possibly, but that's not what's happening here. Adele's tickets are being bought by scalpers who use sophisticated tools to buy up the best seats and resell them at a huge markup.

Ticket scalping was once a shunned practice. But in the age of financial maximization, scalping is mainstream. Value maximization 101.

"A large part of the public has accepted [ticket scalping]," says the manager of Bruce Springsteen, a longtime opponent of the practice. "The negative connotation that used to surround reselling tickets has essentially disappeared." The shift from values to value changed our perspective.

Ticketmaster and even the artists are sometimes in on it. An investigation by the Canadian Broadcasting Corporation found that Ticketmaster builds and markets tools to help scalpers buy tickets in bulk in exchange for extra fees. A *Wall Street Journal* report found that artists and Ticketmaster have collaborated to set aside the best seats and put them up for auction on Ticketmaster's own secondary ticketing website without revealing that the artist and ticket company were doing the selling.

Adele could have easily done something like this. Let the

market do its thing and take your cut of the proceeds. It's great to be popular, right?

But that didn't happen. Because when the market decided who saw her perform, she played for wealthy fans—or less wealthy ones who were spending money they probably shouldn't. As a representative for Tom Waits told *Rolling Stone*: "We don't want to take all of a person's disposable income just to go to one show."

With Adele's considerable power as one of the world's most in-demand performers, she sought a creative solution. Could there be another way?

. . . .

In 2015 Adele announced her first album and tour in four years. Along with it, she announced that for a portion of her tour she would work with a London-based concert listing start-up named Songkick.

Songkick had developed an algorithm that would identify an artist's most "loyal" fans and open up ticket sales just for them. The thinking was twofold: reward the most loyal fans because it's the right thing to do, and because they're the least likely people to resell their tickets.

In select markets, up to 40 percent of Adele's tickets were distributed by Songkick. And it worked. Less than 2 percent of those tickets ended up being scalped, versus ten times that for tickets sold the traditional way. (With many of those tickets going for thousands of dollars.) Songkick's algorithm blocked scalpers and fans got to see the show for a fair price. It's estimated that those loyal fans collectively saved $6.5 million by buying their tickets straight rather than through scalpers.

This was a big win for the fans. But from another perspective it could seem a bit unsettling. A loyalty-measuring algorithm feels like something out of dystopian science fiction. It subverts the age-old policy of first in line gets the tickets. Tech ruining things yet again.

But thanks to tech-empowered scalpers, the old way of doing things had already stopped working. Rather than give in and make her fans pay the scalpers' ransom, Adele tried a different approach.

The algorithm wasn't financially maximizing, it was fairness maximizing. This doesn't mean the tour was some Woodstock 3.0 love-in. People still paid for tickets. The shows still turned a profit. But Adele saw the bigger picture. Her focus wasn't just on how much money she'd make filling stadiums and arenas. It was on who was in those stadiums and arenas, too.

Adele's bold experiment is an example of a Bentoist approach to value. Adele didn't focus just on enriching herself. She saw a broader notion of self-interest. She optimized for her values as a person, as an artist, and as the kind of South London woman who would be more likely to see Adele perform based on loyalty than wealth. This wasn't a Now Me tour, it was a Now Us tour.

With the support of Songkick's algorithm and a Bentoist perspective, Adele did something significant. She found a way to make a rational, values-maximizing choice without money being the goal.

DOWNTOWN

The NBA as we know it began in 1979 with two unrelated but simultaneous events.

The first is well-known. Larry Bird and Magic Johnson, two of the most transcendent stars in NBA history, both started their careers in 1979. Their playmaking skills and epic rivalry made the NBA a phenomenon overnight.

But it's the other event from 1979 that might end up having the longer-term impact: it was the year that the NBA first introduced the three-point shot.

The idea behind the three-pointer was simple: a shot taken from farther away was worth one more point than one taken closer in. But in that first season, only 2.8 three-pointers were attempted each game. Unlike Bird and Magic, the initial impact of the three was negligible.

The three wasn't embraced for a good reason: it was a harder shot to make. Two-point shots went in about half of the time. Three-point shots went in less than 30 percent of the time. The math was clear: it was easier to make twos than threes. So don't shoot threes.

For the first almost thirty years that the three-pointer existed, taking a three was discouraged. Coaches and TV announcers condemned it as selfish. It wasn't how the game was played.

But in the first decade of the 2000s, the way people thought about sports began to change. In the wake of *Moneyball*, the 2003 Michael Lewis book about an underdog baseball team using data analysis to outperform better-resourced competitors, data science became a new focus in sports. Including basketball.

Trailblazing analysts started to ask new questions. Things like: where are the most *efficient* places on the court to shoot?

This was a new kind of question. To know the most efficient shot, new forms of measurement were needed. To get the necessary data, new kinds of technology were required. Soon, teams began using special cameras to scan all the action on the court.

Analysts and algorithms categorized and measured each play with intense granularity. They tracked not just whether a shot went in. They looked at precisely where on the court that player was. Whether the player had dribbled before shooting or had just caught a pass. Who the nearest defender was, how close they were, and how tall they were. No detail was too small.

When the analysts added up the data, the results differed greatly from the conventional wisdom. It turned out that other than a layup or dunk, the best shot was a three. A new statistic, called "effective field goal percentage," showed that teams taking threes would miss more shots but would also—counterintuitively—score more points in the long run.

For decades people saw the basketball court as a set configuration of events. There were good shots and bad shots. Things you did and didn't do. And suddenly those conventions were put into question by a new definition of value. According to this new way of seeing things, how we'd been playing the game was all wrong.

The basketball establishment was understandably skeptical.

Effective field goal percentages by shot location

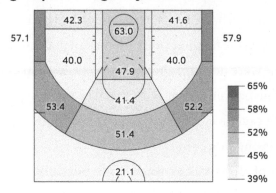

SOURCE: CHANG, MAHESWARAN, SU, KWOK, LEVY, WEXLER, SQUIRE 2014, "QUANTIFYING SHOT QUALITY IN THE NBA"

Computers telling us how to play? No, thanks. But a few teams tried shooting more threes and outperformed expectations. Others followed their lead. Within a decade, basketball was transformed. There were more three-pointers taken in the 2017–18 NBA season alone than in all of the 1980s combined.

When we discover new forms of value, it changes how we play the game.

DODGING THE MULLET

Adele and the NBA analysts were looking for better ways to get from point A to point B. Adele wanted to put on a great show for fans. NBA teams wanted to win basketball games. Was there a different way than what everyone else was doing? In seeking other possibilities, they uncovered deeper understandings of value.

When Adele found an algorithm that would help her most

loyal fans see her play, she was in pursuit of community, not money. When NBA teams started shooting threes, they were optimizing for winning the game rather than making a basket.

These were not easy choices to make. It wasn't just about now. It wasn't just about them. In both cases the new value required a near-term sacrifice. It meant making less money from the tour. It meant missing more shots.

Both of these values were made possible by the forces that transformed health: technology, measurement, and specificity. The algorithm Adele used was made possible by technology. Measuring loyalty is similar to the data-driven strategies used to sell ads and make e-commerce recommendations. Songkick evolved these tools to fit a specific-use case: a musician and her fans. The data-driven emergence of the three-pointer is similar. Analysts used measurement to find the best places on the court to shoot, then evolved their games to amplify those values.

Also like medicine and health, these new values were (and still are) criticized by the status quo.

The three-pointer was viewed as a gimmick. Not real basketball. Adele's ticket strategy was criticized by many in the music industry as irrational, pointless, and even conceited. Who are *you* to fight the forces of the market? Behind closed doors, the monopolist ticketing and touring company Live Nation pressured other artists not to follow her lead.

Adele was turning her back on the dominant values. She wasn't looking for a new tool to squeeze more money out of her fans. She looked outside the system for one to help her do just the opposite. From the mind-set of classic rational self-interest, this was irrational. But based on Adele's values, it was perfectly rational.

Imagine that Adele didn't make this choice. Imagine that, like other artists, she partnered with the ticketing companies and took a cut of the scalped tickets.

According to the mind-set of financial maximization, this would be ideal. When people can spend as much money as they want to see Adele, the market is operating efficiently. This is the natural, value-maximizing way things should work.

But this choice would also cause Adele to create a Mullet Economy with her very own fans.

Think about it. Adele's fans spending more money to see her perform creates a lot more income for Adele and a lot less income for them. Higher ticket prices aren't a distant economic concept. It's money that comes out of the bank accounts of fans who often have much less than the artist they love.

It's not like more people see Adele play if tickets cost more. It's the same number of people either way. Unless you're a ticket scalper or rich enough to buy front-row seats, there's little upside. It's the Mullet Economy on a human scale.

It may seem like Adele is making an altruistic choice, but that discounts the sophistication of what she's doing. She's not doing this from a pure heart. She's doing this to achieve a challenging and specific outcome: arenas full of people coming together for a communal and fair experience. Adele is maximizing and optimizing for a different set of values.

When we find the courage to embrace a wider sense of value, the impact can be significant. Even if it's just one day a week.

CLOSED ON SUNDAYS

Balancing the influence of money isn't some hip #resistance act. The history of restricting money's reach goes back much further than that.

Think of the Sabbath. Both Christianity and Judaism use the Sabbath as a structural break to preserve time for rest and worship. It creates space for values to exist without dictating what those values must be, only what they *can't* be: more work. The Sabbath is a clever way to create space beyond the reach of money.

For many years in America, the Sabbath was enforced with "blue laws" that prohibited stores from opening on Sundays. While the origin of Sunday as a rest day was Christian, blue laws also found support from unions and others who saw it as positive for public life. Sundays were preserved as a universal public (lowercase) holy day.

Today, most blue laws have been reversed, and for many people, the idea of Sunday as holy seems like ancient history. Sundays are for sports, weekend getaways, and getting errands done. Only the devoutly religious still believe that Sundays should be preserved for sacred nourishment.

But the Sabbath as a check on money hasn't completely

vanished from public life. In fact, the most highly rated fast-food chain in America, Chick-fil-A, closes on Sundays. It's one of the only major chains in America that still does.

Chick-fil-A closes on Sundays because of the beliefs of its late founder, S. Truett Cathy. In the 1940s he closed his original twenty-four-hour diner on Sundays so employees could have a day off. Chick-fil-A continues to follow this tradition today.

This comes at a real cost. Being closed on Sundays means 14 percent less time open each week. That works out to nearly two months a year that Chick-fil-A is closed while the competition is open. As a values-minded establishment, Chick-fil-A is exactly the kind of place that churchgoing people want to go on Sundays. And after-church lunch is big business.

It's estimated that being closed on Sundays costs Chick-fil-A more than $1 billion a year. Despite being a for-profit company that wants to grow and succeed in the ways companies want to grow and succeed, and despite the billion-dollar price tag, Chick-fil-A stays closed on Sundays.

A Maximizing Class consultant would look at this and say this is madness. Look at how much money you're leaving on the table. You're not maximizing. But Chick-fil-A's leadership might answer that they are maximizing—for multiple values, not just one. Yes, they're a for-profit fast-food company. But they also believe in tradition, and they're willing to make a billion dollars less a year because of that.

To the financially maximizing mind-set, this is irrational. But from a Bentoist perspective, it's completely rational. Chick-fil-A is choosing, in a defined way, to optimize for values other than money. Not every day. Just on Sundays.

There are literal costs to this but benefits, too. Chick-fil-A is one of America's most popular restaurant chains and top-ranked places to work. The company's unique commitment to its values is a big reason why.

REBELS ON A BUDGET

Sometimes it's what you *don't* do that creates value.

For members of the Financial Independence Retire Early movement (FIRE), maximizing value means *not* spending money on things they don't need. Wasting money is for losers.

FIRE is a personal finance strategy that teaches people how to minimize their spending and maximize their long-term goals. For FIRE followers, a key first-date question is less "How much do you make?" and more "How much do you save?"

According to FIRE thinking, the point of money isn't to get rich and buy nice things. The point of money is to create the security to focus on real value in life. FIRE is Maslow's hierarchy of needs executed with precision. As a popular FIRE writer named Peter Adeney writes on his blog, *Mr. Money Mustache*:

"By focusing on happiness itself, you can lead a *much better life* than those who focus on convenience, luxury, and following the lead of the financially illiterate herd . . . Happiness comes from many sources, but none of these sources involve car or purse upgrades."

There's no single figure, organization, or proprietary algorithm at the heart of FIRE. It's spread through blogs, books, and shared Excel spreadsheets. The tools and strategies are created, tested, and iterated on by members of the community.

Followers of FIRE tend to be Millennials. People for whom the American dream of comfort, convenience, and excess seems out of reach and out of touch. They're creating a new kind of dream instead.

"We've just chosen to live far below our means," says one FIRE follower. "That itself is a radical idea."

As the *New York Times* writes about a thirty-three-year-old woman who changed her life to fit the principles of FIRE:

"Ms. Rieckens, who works in recruiting, was initially reluctant to give up her BMW and beachy life and the prestige that went with it, until she saw a retirement calculator that showed they could retire in 10 years if they adopted FIRE and moved, or when they are 90 if they continued their upscale lifestyle."

FIRE followers are equipped with heightened long-term awareness. By looking at the present through its ultimate consequences, they bring their Now Me choices in line with their Future Me values and goals.

This heightened awareness leads FIRE followers to diverge from the pack.

While the population living in cities continues to grow, FIRE followers tend to live in suburban and rural areas. The high costs of living in top cities are an expense that FIRE followers learn to cut. While carbon and consumer consumption continue to rise, FIRE followers seek to cut their energy use and spending to unlock their financial freedom. FIRE is like Thoreau's *Walden* except with iPhones and a Tyler Durden edge.

While FIRE followers are driven by a Future Me goal—creating a sustainable life—getting there means paying close attention to Now Me. By living on a budget and treating money with more respect than their free-spending peers.

Is the dream of early retirement realistic for everyone? Probably not. On a minimum-wage salary, saving meaningful money is very hard no matter how little someone spends. But another way of thinking about money is useful for everyone. FIRE separates money and happiness, revealing their inconsistent connection while respecting both for the value they bring.

Limiting the dominance of financial maximization doesn't mean ignoring money, it means putting it into context. FIRE followers are very money conscious. They respect its importance. They understand where it creates value. But they also understand that money is not the only value that matters.

BENTOISM IRL

Expanding the value spectrum beyond financial maximization isn't a pipe dream. We're already doing it. Adele's ticket sales algorithm, Chick-fil-A's hours, the FIRE movement, and the rise of the three-pointer are all examples of Bentoist values already happening in real life.

In each of these examples, people are rationally thinking about all areas of their self-interest. They're considering their future selves, people around them, and their current needs.

Are shifts like these just window dressing or do they actually matter? I speak from experience: yes, they do.

When Kickstarter became a public benefit corporation in 2015, it was as if the company shifted Bentos. As a traditionally structured for-profit company, Kickstarter was expected to think only about its Now Me needs—profitability and the interests of shareholders. But by becoming a PBC, Kickstarter was codifying and committing to what its Now Us, Future Me, and Future Us values said it should do, too.

Becoming a PBC reflected the values that Kickstarter had always had. But those same values put us at some theoretical risk as a traditionally structured for-profit company. Theoretically our public statements about not wanting to sell or go public could have led to a shareholder suing because these decisions meant we were not open to all forms of maximizing shareholder value.

Something like this happening was extremely unlikely, but there is precedent: in 2000, Ben & Jerry's board of directors was pressured to sell the company to Unilever over the founders' objections. If Ben & Jerry's had declined the offer, investors were threatening to sue, accusing the board members of neglecting their fiduciary obligations. Even though Ben & Jerry's' values were central to its brand and identity, they had no standing compared to shareholders' legally backed demands.

As a PBC, on the other hand, Kickstarter's mission and commitments are embedded in the company's legal foundation. Kickstarter's PBC charter lays out fifteen commitments. They include pledges to:

- "Not use loopholes or other esoteric but legal tax management strategies to reduce [the company's] tax burden"
- "Not lobby or campaign for public policies unless they align with [the company's] mission and values, regardless of possible economic benefits to the company"
- "Always support, serve, and champion artists and creators, especially those working in less commercial areas"
- "Engage beyond [the company's] walls with the greater issues and conversations affecting artists and creators"
- "Donate 5% of its after-tax profit towards arts and music education, and to organizations fighting to end systemic inequality"

These commitments established redlines for how Kickstarter must always behave. The values they represent aren't vague platitudes. They have teeth.

Within a year of becoming a PBC, Kickstarter began publishing a new, separate website called The Creative Independent.

The Creative Independent is a growing resource of practical

and emotional advice for creative people. It publishes an interview or essay every weekday from artists and creators about their practice and its challenges. Its ultimate ambition is to become a kind of Wikipedia for creativity.

The Creative Independent has no advertising, charges nothing for its content, and has a full-time staff. Kickstarter pays for all of it. And yet there's no Kickstarter logo anywhere. Kickstarter is listed in the site's footer as its publisher, but otherwise derives no direct benefit.

So why do it?

Because The Creative Independent is a value-creating project according to the commitments in Kickstarter's PBC charter. The site supports the creative community, provides resources and educational material for creative people, and elevates the work of artists and creators. These are values that Kickstarter is committed to growing, and The Creative Independent supports with distinction. The Creative Independent—or other similarly focused projects Kickstarter may develop in the future—doesn't need to make money to make value.

PATAGONIA, TESLA, AND FUTURE US

Few companies are more radical in their approach to corporate governance than the clothing maker Patagonia. Patagonia offers free in-office child care (since 1983), promises lifetime repairs for its clothing (one of its facilities repairs thirty thousand pieces a year), and treats its employees as fellow human beings (as the title of founder Yvon Chouinard's remarkable book, *Let My People Go Surfing*, suggests).

Patagonia does all of this and more while being a profitable, successful, and beloved business.

Patagonia was one of the first companies to become a public benefit corporation. Its PBC charter includes an amazing pledge about competition. It reads:

"In support of our commitment to 'use business to inspire and implement solutions to the environmental crisis,' we will share proprietary information and best practices with other businesses, including direct competitors, when the board of directors determines that doing so may produce a material positive impact on the environment."

If Patagonia creates some new way to manufacture clothes that's better for the planet, it won't just keep it for itself. It'll share that information with its direct competitors. This is a policy optimizing for Future Us. It's something the company has already followed through on, too.

In 2014 Patagonia released a new biorubber for wet suits after spending four years developing a more sustainable fiber. After making this significant investment, what did Patagonia do? It shared the material with its competitors. An ad announcing the decision reads: "We have the best weed in town (and we're giving it away)."

According to the Now Me perspective, this makes little sense. But as a Future Us–maximizing decision, it makes perfect sense.

This may make Patagonia sound like a charity, but it's not. It's a for-profit public benefit corporation with challenges and competitors just like everybody else. But Patagonia also sees the big picture. Its Now Me needs must be met, but Patagonia balances the here and now with significant investments into Future Us.

■ ■ ■ ■

While not a public benefit corporation, Tesla offers another example of Future Us thinking. Not just the fact that the company makes electric cars. The way it goes about it.

In 2015, Tesla announced that it was making all of its patents—the intellectual property that underlies its technology—fully public for any company to use. Rather than protect these ideas, it decided to give them away.

Why do this? Why not license those patents to other carmakers? Because the goal wasn't for Tesla to make more money. The goal was for electric cars to become more common. Tesla was willing to give away its best ideas to help make that happen.

"Given that annual new vehicle production is approaching 100 million per year and the global fleet is approximately 2 billion cars, it is impossible for Tesla to build electric cars fast enough to address the carbon crisis," Tesla CEO Elon Musk wrote. "By the same token, it means the market is enormous. Our true competition is not the small trickle of non-Tesla electric cars being produced, but rather the enormous flood of gasoline cars pouring out of the world's factories every day."

Rather than maximizing for a Now Me financial return, Tesla's patent strategy maximizes for Future Us sustainability. Selling cars isn't the priority. Electric cars becoming the norm is the priority.

Patagonia's and Tesla's focus on Future Us makes them outliers right now. But they may not be outliers for much longer.

POP BENTOS

These real-life examples of Bentoism come from mainstream people with Main Street values. People at the top of their fields trying to do better. People trying to win at sports. People with strong religious beliefs. People trying to save money. People trying to protect life on Earth. They're about as wholesome as it gets.

These people are making a difference in the world. Their curiosity and bold choices are inching us forward. Most of these value-based choices are morally rooted, but not all of them. Teams shooting three-pointers aren't trying to right some wrong. They're looking for a better way to win.

Bentoism doesn't force any specific values beyond a greater awareness of what's going on. You can be a fast-food chain and make a Bentoist choice. You can be an environmentalist and make a Bentoist choice. You can live off-grid or you can be a pop star. You can be a Christian or a Muslim. Bentoism doesn't tell you who to be. It helps you see how your own values line up with the situation at hand, and empowers you to make more self-coherent, values-based choices.

This way of thinking is growing.

As I write this, the country-turned-pop star Taylor Swift has signed a new major label record deal. In her negotiations, she got the label to make a fascinating concession. Here's how Swift describes it in an Instagram post:

"There was one condition that meant more to me than any other deal point. As part of my new contract with Universal Music Group, I asked that any sale of their Spotify shares result in a distribution of money to their artists, non-recoupable. They have generously agreed to this, at what they believe will be much better terms than paid out previously by majors. I see this as a sign that we are heading towards positive change for creators—a goal I'm never going to stop trying to help achieve, in whatever ways I can."

Taylor Swift used her clout to not just negotiate a lucrative contract for herself (which she did), she used it to negotiate something on behalf of thousands of other artists, too. Like Adele, Taylor Swift isn't acting on just Now Me. She's intentionally creating value in Now Us and Future Us, too.

You might say, well, this is easy for someone like Taylor Swift or Adele. They're already rich and famous. It doesn't cost them anything. And it's easy for Chick-fil-A, Kickstarter, Patagonia, and Tesla to act in generous ways. They're already successful, too.

There's something to that. To go back to Maslow's hierarchy, these are people and organizations that have fulfilled their safety and security needs. They can afford to be more generous and more long-term oriented because they aren't facing profound existential threats every day.

But what if their focus beyond financial value has been the secret to their success all along? What if growing and optimizing for nonfinancial values isn't some radical, out-there thing? What if it's simply the better way to do things? What if it's the world around us that's radical and out-there, and it's choices like these that can—slowly but surely—bring our values back?

That's the potential of a Bentoist perspective. Not to turn back the clock, but to finally turn it forward. How long is that going to take?

CHAPTER NINE

HOW TO DO A
PERFECT HANDSTAND

FOR THE PAST TWENTY YEARS, JEFF BEZOS, THE FOUNDER and CEO of Amazon, has published an annual letter to the company's shareholders. These letters contain information about the company's performance, strategy, and goals.

In the 2017 letter, Bezos shares an interesting story about handstands. He writes:

> A close friend recently decided to learn to do a perfect free-standing handstand. No leaning against a wall. Not for just a few seconds. Instagram good. She decided to start her journey by taking a handstand workshop at her yoga studio. She then practiced for a while but wasn't getting the results she wanted. So, she hired a handstand coach. Yes, I know what you're thinking, but evidently this is an actual thing that

exists. In the very first lesson, the coach gave her some wonderful advice. "Most people," he said, "think that if they work hard, they should be able to master a handstand in about two weeks. The reality is that it takes about six months of daily practice. If you think you should be able to do it in two weeks, you're just going to end up quitting." Unrealistic beliefs on scope—often hidden and undiscussed—kill high standards. To achieve high standards yourself or as part of a team, you need to form and proactively communicate realistic beliefs about how hard something is going to be.

When we underestimate how long and how much effort it will take to do things, we cut corners. We give up. And when things don't work out, we wonder what went wrong. But when we're realistic in our expectations and make a plan to get where we want to go, we've got a shot.

If it takes six months of daily practice to do a perfect handstand, how long does it take for the world to change?

THE THIRTY-YEAR THEORY OF CHANGE

We want change to be instant. Immediate. But there is biological, historical, and sociological evidence that suggests thirty years is the right amount of time to think about substantive change.

By "substantive change" I mean significant movement in the majority point of view. A paradigm shift where a previously new idea becomes an accepted default. Changes like these happen all the time. But they take time to happen. About thirty years, more or less.

What kinds of changes am I talking about? I don't mean the emergence of a new product. I mean significant shifts in values, beliefs, and behavior.

Take the antiseptic method.

In 1867 Joseph Lister shared the positive findings of his new technique in *The Lancet*, the most important medical journal. Did the medical establishment rally around him? Not at all. That same journal printed pointed criticism of his methods not long after. In 1881, President Garfield's doctors ignored Lister's recommendations even after one of them saw an in-person demonstration by Lister himself.

And yet in 1903 when the king of England needed an emergency appendectomy, his doctors called Lister. They followed Lister's method and the king survived. King Edward later told him, "I know that if it had not been for you and your work, I wouldn't be sitting here today."

Lister's treatment wasn't considered reputable enough for the dying American president, but doctors for the British monarch sought it out a few years later. From controversial to caring for the life of the king in thirty years.

How about the three-point shot?

The three-pointer was added to the NBA in 1979, but was not heavily utilized. It wasn't how the game was played. Thirty years later, new metrics encouraged teams to shoot more threes for the first time. The three-pointer was no longer a new part of the game.

It was normal. It went from new to essential in thirty years, and now we can't imagine basketball any other way.

How about financial maximization?

Milton Friedman's 1970 *New York Times* essay introduced financial maximization to the mainstream. "The social responsibility of business is profit," he announced. Businesses got the message, and society did, too. Getting rich went from essential for 36 percent of incoming college students in 1970 to essential for more than 70 percent of them in 2000. In thirty years, this new mindset went from fringe to dominant.

There's something to thirty years as a cadence for change.

GENERATIONAL CHANGE

"[Imagine] what the social life of humankind would be like if one generation lived on forever and none followed to replace it," Hungarian philosopher Karl Mannheim wrote in 1928. In that world, society's values and norms would remain constant.

In contrast, Mannheim says that in our own society:

(A) new participants in the cultural process are emerging, whilst

(B) former participants in that process are continually disappearing;

(C) members of any one generation can participate only in a temporally limited section of the historical process.

In other words, as new people are born and existing people die, things change. Death is life's natural transition of values and power. We each feature in a few scenes of a much bigger ensemble story. Mannheim writes that because of our temporary roles:

(D) it is therefore necessary continually to transmit the accumulated cultural heritage;

(E) the transition from generation to generation is a continuous process.

To maintain order and build on the progress that's already been made, we continuously transfer knowledge and values from one generation to the next.

Imagine life as a party where new people are constantly arriving, existing people are constantly leaving, and the festivities keep going. The party keeps going because "the accumulated cultural heritage" is continuously transferred from one set of partygoers to the next.

When people first arrive they're shown where to put their jacket, where to find food, and the drinks in the kitchen. The newcomers stay wallflowers until they get their bearings, then join the fray. This is life from childhood to adolescence to the start of adulthood (ages zero to thirty).

Those in adulthood (ages thirty to sixty) control the party. They pick the music and make the rules. But they can't run the show forever. The dance floor gets tiring and new people keep trying to take over anyway.

When someone's had enough, they take a break in a quieter room (age sixty or so and over) before leaving the party altogether (you-know-what). *Their* party ends, but the party itself keeps going. The next generation steps onto the dance floor as fresh arrivals learn the ropes.

This is the world. Existing people leave, new people arrive, and the party keeps going. And growing. Every second 1.8 people die and 4.3 people are born. The global population is growing 1.06 percent a year.

A 1 percent growth rate would get many CEOs fired, but compound interest combined with the inevitability of death means a lot of turnover in a relatively short amount of time. People alive today will be a minority of the total people alive thirty years from now. In thirty years, a third of the people alive now will be dead and half of the larger population will be new.

If the party worked this way, with two people leaving and four new people arriving each minute, the makeup of the room would change quickly. What's normal would change with it.

Your impressions of the party are shaped by what the party is like when you first get there. People who were teenagers at the same time tend to view the world similarly. That first impression is the baseline of normal that the rest of life filters through.

For anyone who experienced life before the iPhone (which dates back to only 2008), they're aware of the "newness" of this

presence in our lives. Just as someone who lived through the intro-duction of television could better see its effects.

The generations growing up now are the first for whom the presence of smartphones isn't novel. It just *is*. Their values regard-ing technology will differ from earlier generations simply because it was already ubiquitous when they were born.

For my three-year-old son, seeing an electric car charging is normal. For his forty-year-old father, it's novel. I experienced the first 90 percent of my life without electric cars. He, thankfully, will not.

It's the same for all of us who have grown up in a world of financial maximization. It feels like this song has been playing forever, but it hasn't. That's just how things were when we got to the party.

■ ■ ■ ■

Transferring values, Mannheim writes, "is a continuous pro-cess." Continuous doesn't mean harmonious, but it does mean that change tends to be gradual. The antiseptic method is a good example.

When Joseph Lister proposed his idea of sterilizing wounds, it was a new argument based on the also-new science of germ the-ory. It was met with hostility. For an established surgeon to con-form to these new methods would require a kind of self-negation that many doctors found hard to do. In all likelihood so would we.

But for doctors and scientists in training at the time of Lister's proposal, the antiseptic method was easier to accept. They saw how the results justified the treatment, rather than feeling personally judged by them. Buying into the antiseptic method didn't require a deep rewiring of their beliefs. Their reputations weren't on the line.

Even after Lister published his encouraging findings in *The Lancet*, adoption was gradual and debated. In Glasgow, where Lister lived and practiced, mortality rates from surgery declined slowly. But his methods outlasted his critics.

Thirty years later enough of the older generation of surgeons had died, stopped practicing, or been marginalized for their outdated thinking that their influence had waned. A younger generation who accepted the science of the antiseptic method was practicing in their place. The changing of the guard created a tipping point. The antiseptic method became accepted science and the majority point of view, and it took about thirty years to get there.

If a significant change is successful—even something as consequential as dramatically improving surgical mortality rates—it takes time for that change to become the new norm. The new idea must prove itself to—and ultimately outlast—its skeptics. When it does, the new becomes normal.

EXERCISE

In 1960, the future president of the United States called out America for being fat. It wasn't pre-Twitter Trump. It was President-Elect

John F. Kennedy in a *Sports Illustrated* essay called "The Soft American."

Kennedy pointed out that in 1951, 51 percent of Yale freshmen passed a basic physical fitness test. But by 1960, just 35 percent passed. What had happened to vigorous, young America?

In a word: television.

In 1950, there were 3 million TVs in the United States. By the end of the decade there were more than 50 million of them. And millions of new couch potatoes and extra pounds along with them. Life had become leisurely. The good times had become too good.

The change so worried Kennedy that he made fitness a national priority. He instituted national fitness guidelines, created a presidential commission on physical fitness, and even challenged the military to march fifty miles in twenty hours (later called the Kennedy Hike) to prove itself.

From the pulpit of the presidency, Kennedy gave America a new national priority and pastime: to exercise. As crazy as it sounds, this was a new idea.

"In the forties and fifties, casual interest in nutrition, physical fitness, and obtaining one's best physical shape were not popular subjects," writes former Mr. California Harold Zinkin, a central figure of Muscle Beach and the history of exercise. According to Zinkin, Kennedy's 1960 call for fitness "even then felt revolutionary." This from one of the few people who actually worked out.

At the time, strenuous exercise was considered dangerous and unhealthy.

"Doctors warned against lifting weights, telling people it was bad for their health," Arnold Schwarzenegger wrote about weight lifting in the 1960s. "Even some professional athletes avoided the gym, because of myths that lifting weights would make them musclebound and less mobile."

In the 1960s someone running outside for exercise was so out of the ordinary that people called the police. Strom Thurmond, the South Carolina segregationist, was stopped by police while running in 1968.

The running trend began to grow after a small book called *Jogging* introduced a gentler style of running in 1966. Jogging had recently been introduced in New Zealand, where the book's author, running coach Bill Bowerman, experienced it for himself. The book sold a million copies, and Bowerman designed a new running shoe for the growing community and cofounded a company to make it, called Nike.

By the late 1960s, the *Chicago Tribune*, *Saturday Evening Post*, and *New York Times* all reported on the curious phenomenon of people running outside for pleasure and health.

It wasn't the only new exercise trend.

In California, a new hot spot named Gold's Gym was making weight lifting mainstream. Started in 1965 by one of the original Muscle Beach weightlifters, the Gold's chain put serious exercise within reach of millions of Americans for the first time. By 1972 1.7 million Americans belonged to a gym. At the end of the decade it would be ten times that many.

Aerobics, a new style of exercise, invented by an air force

physiologist and physical therapist, was introduced in 1968. By the 1980s Jane Fonda was leading tens of millions of aerobic routines on VHS players in basements, bedrooms, and living rooms across America.

Exercise went from revolutionary in 1960 to normal thirty years later. In 1993, a generation after Kennedy's call to exercise, America had its first jogging president. Today 60 million Americans belong to a gym. Twenty million Americans do yoga. A half million people run marathons each year. Exercise as a pastime has grown from nothing to normal in an amazingly short amount of time.

We don't think of exercise as a success because we don't recognize how new it is in its modern form.

FROM NEW TO NORMAL

Change happens in response to a crisis. The rise of television inspired the rise of exercise. Lister experimented with antiseptics because people kept dying after surgery. Without the disease, there's no need for the cure.

Case in point: recycling.

The idea of throwing something "away" when you're done with it is a twentieth-century concept. Packaging is a recent thing. Until the twentieth century, very little was meant to be discarded. Things were recycled by default.

It didn't take long for society to feel the effects of the increasing amounts of garbage created by its new consumerist culture. In

1953 the Keep America Beautiful campaign started to combat the new problem of littering. By the end of the 1960s—after just two decades of the new good life—America's accumulating piles of garbage had become hard to ignore.

In response, Oregon started the first modern recycling program in 1970. In 1980 Woodbury, New Jersey, became the first city to mandate recycling. This decision looked even better after a barge of New York City trash was stranded at sea in the late 1980s and nobody was willing to take it. At the time New York City recycled just 1 percent of its garbage. A crisis moment had arrived.

Recycling became mandatory in an increasing number of cities in the 1990s and early 2000s (though, as we've learned, many used the problematic single-stream method) and grew as a business and everyday household chore. Half of Americans recycle today after very few recycled a generation ago (and essentially everyone did just two generations before that in pre-consumerist times).

Organic food's story is similar. Concern over pesticides and processed food created a rising interest in higher-quality food.

Early on, organic food grew through health food stores and independent retailers. (I vividly remember going with my mom to our small, local health food store in the 1980s.) It became much more common after the Food and Drug Administration set standards defining organic food in 2000.

Today organic food is common and widely available. A third of Americans intentionally shop for it. There's an organic section in Walmart.

Recycling, organic food, and exercise may not be *the* mainstream, but they *are* mainstream. In thirty years each went from a new idea to a new default. And they're not done growing yet.

CHANGE IS NOT ALWAYS PROGRESS

As encouraging as trends like these are, we should also be cautious in our assessment of change.

We tend to assume that what's new must be improved. That technology means progress. It's a mistake advertising campaigns spend billions to help us make.

New *can* mean better and technology *can* create progress. But those things don't automatically go together. Other times they can be "improved means to an unimproved end," as Thoreau put it in *Walden*.

Consider that we spend billions of dollars a year on bottled water when we've never had more readily available clean and free water in postindustrial history.

As tap water has gotten better, we've drunk less of it. Bottled water marketing convinced us that tap water is substandard and old-fashioned. "When we're done, tap water will be relegated to showers and washing dishes," a beverage executive said in 2000.

Introduced in the 1980s and previously a public resource, bottled water was the top-selling beverage in the United States thirty years later. Sales continue to grow 10 percent a year while the free stuff in the taps is increasingly unused—and less available.

The commercialization of water coincided with the vanishing of public drinking fountains—a mainstay of public life for centuries. The disappearance is so pronounced that a 2018 announcement that London would build twenty new drinking fountains was met with sincere but depressing exuberance.

Just as change is not always progress, we also have to remember that progress is not inevitable. Progress is earned.

These brief overviews on the rise of exercise, recycling, and organic food may create the impression that these changes were natural and inevitable. That they just organically happened. But that's not the case.

These changes happened because people worked hard to make them happen. People advocated for a new perspective, first making it real in their own lives and gradually expanding it to others. These ideas found a community of supporters and institutional partners that helped onboard them to the mainstream.

For the world to change in a specific direction people have to make it happen. If a new idea can create value and win over others, it has a shot. But this outcome is far from guaranteed.

2050

Which brings us all the way back to 2050.

At the start of the book I asked where we will be in 2050. This isn't just a round number. It's thirty years from now. A generation away from this moment.

Thirty years. That's how long it took for exercise, organic

food, recycling, the three-pointer, sterilized surgery, the internet, and so many other unnoticed, normal parts of life to go from new idea to normal. A lot can change in thirty years. If a Bentoist movement were to continue to grow, thirty years from now—2050—is when we might expect a noticeable shift in how we think about value. But we also need realistic expectations about the nature of change.

Change is not overnight. Change is incremental. A lot changes over the long term, but instant results are harder to come by.

Change isn't a sprint. It's a marathon—*and* a relay. Each person or generation runs a leg of a longer race. The finish line may not appear in our lifetimes. This is no reason to feel discouraged. It's simply the math we have to work with. Change isn't impossible. It simply takes time. No matter how hard we try, we're not going to do a perfect handstand in a day.

But once change starts to grow, it can accelerate quickly. Change is contagious. Change creates compound interest: some people changing means more people will change. A growing movement can seem to tip overnight in favor of a new idea. On a long enough timeline, anything is possible.

We should also be aware of how much harder change is when it means you have to do the changing. We may scoff at the doctors who ignored germ theory, but nobody likes having to change when changing isn't their idea. It's a hard thing for our egos to deal with.

That's why serious changes to address climate change will ultimately come from generations who have less responsibility for the crisis. It's easier to fix somebody else's problems than your own. Even in the sweeping forces of history, human nature still plays a starring role.

GENERATIONAL CLICK

In 1983, legendary science-fiction author Isaac Asimov was asked what the year 2019 would be like. At the time, this was thirty-five years away.

Among other things, Asimov predicted growing joblessness due to automation and a resulting shift in the structure of work and society. The challenges would be bigger and more challenging than the Industrial Revolution, he speculated.

But soon, he said, this would change: "The generation of the transition will be dying out, and there will be a new generation growing up who will have been educated into the new world. It is quite likely that society, then, will have entered a phase that may be more or less permanently improved over the situation as it now exists."

Sometimes a generation and a moment click. They're ideally suited to take on the challenge of their time. That's why people celebrate the Greatest Generation, those who fought World War II. In a moment of crisis, a generation of regular people from around the world were ready to stand up for the values of society.

Asimov seems to predict a similar click between the challenges of our transition into "the new world" and the generation that would be coming up right about now. This would be the moment, Asimov predicted, that everything could change.

CHAPTER TEN

VALUES MAXIMIZING CLASS

FEW PEOPLE IN HISTORY CAN TAKE CREDIT FOR CREATING as much economic growth as John Maynard Keynes. The British economist was the founder of macroeconomics and a key architect of the global economy. During the Great Depression he successfully convinced world governments to spend public funds to create jobs and other forms of social support. Maybe you've heard someone say "Keynesian economics" on a podcast before. They meant this guy.

Keynes was a great champion of capitalism. In a 1930 essay called "Economic Possibilities for Our Grandchildren," he points out that from 2000 BCE until 1700 CE (aka the bloodletting era) there was little economic growth or technological development in the world. During those thousands of years, he estimates, life got 1 percent better—at most.

But then, writes Keynes, this started to change. When Spain sent ships across the Atlantic in the sixteenth century, they discovered not just the New World. They discovered the magic of what came to be called capitalism. Investments into New World expeditions brought lucrative financial returns that were invested into further expeditions that brought further lucrative returns and on and on. This was the eureka moment when humanity discovered the dual powers of capital reinvestment and compound interest.

To be clear, these expeditions weren't just simple and benign trade exchanges. There *were* trade exchanges, but there was also the exploitation and genocide of millions of people and the destruction of countless ways of life. Along with financial returns, the ugliest parts of capitalism were there from the beginning.

For all his passion for capitalism, Keynes saw its limitations. In the same essay, he writes:

"When the accumulation of wealth is no longer of high social importance, there will be great changes in the code of morals. We shall be able to rid ourselves of many of the pseudo-moral principles which have hag-ridden us for two hundred years, by which we have exalted some of the most distasteful of human qualities into the position of the highest virtues. We shall be able to afford to dare to assess the money-motive at its true value. The love of money as a possession—as distinguished from the love of money as a means to the enjoyments and realities of life—will be recognised for what it is, a somewhat disgusting morbidity."

Despite this, Keynes wasn't proposing to do anything about it. Not yet.

"But beware! The time for all this is not yet. For at least another hundred years we must pretend to ourselves and to everyone that fair is foul and foul is fair; for foul is useful and fair is not. Avarice and usury and precaution must be our gods for a little longer still. For only they can lead us out of the tunnel of economic necessity into daylight."

To keep the economic growth going, Keynes writes, we should pretend that greed, envy, and other "foul" emotions are good "for at least another hundred years." By then, Keynes thought, there would be enough wealth to leave this duplicity behind.

Keynes wrote these words in 1930. Which means we're just about one hundred years from then. After a century of people pretending "fair is foul and foul is fair," these "gods," as Keynes calls them, have overtaken us.

But the dominance of money is not forever. Not even Keynes thought so. Right now is the moment the man who invented macroeconomics predicted we might escape "the tunnel of economic necessity into daylight."

This means us.

THE PATH NOT TAKEN

In the decades following Keynes's words, avarice, usury, and precaution brought prosperity.

From 1946 to 1973, American workers experienced the greatest period of wage growth in history. Median pay increased 91 percent and the average family's real income more than doubled.

America built the infrastructure of its future, most importantly a growing middle class, all while people worked less and had disposable income for the first time. The goal was prosperity for all, and everyone was on board.

And then financial maximization took the wheel.

Under financial maximization, the goal of broad prosperity disappeared. Instead it became about *my* prosperity. The national default went from growing the middle class (growth for Now and Future Us) to financial maximization (growth for Me and only Me).

Forty years later, the United States has the highest wealth inequality in the world and the American middle class—a central focus during America's boom—is shrinking. The average employee's pay (adjusted for inflation) has been nearly flat since 1973. The average CEO, meanwhile, makes 271 times more than the average worker.

After enjoying the highest standard of living in the world for essentially the entire twentieth century, the United States fell to seventeenth in 2018. Since financial maximization took over:

- Public services and infrastructure have fallen into disrepair
- Monopolies block competition and entrepreneurship
- Chains starve local communities of money and opportunity
- Corporations and the wealthy hide an estimated 10 percent of GDP in offshore tax havens
- Politicians rewrite laws to help big business at the public's expense

Had America continued along its pre-financial-maximization trajectory, today:

- The average worker would get paid more
- CEOs and executives would make less, but still be among the highest-paid people on the planet
- Taxes for top earners would be higher
- Public services, infrastructure, and education would be better funded
- The rich would still be rich, just not *as* rich

In other words, a stronger civil society than we have today. Because of financial maximization, this seems like a pipe dream. But it isn't. That world existed before and something like it can exist again.

Getting there requires a change in values. This starts by relearning how to see beyond our Now Me self-interest.

Some will argue that looking beyond their Now Me is irrational and unreasonable. The world is a jungle, the argument goes. When push comes to shove, people will do whatever it takes to survive. It's everybody for themselves.

We've seen the story in so many summer blockbusters and played it in so many first-person shooters that we believe it. Once bad stuff starts going down—which could be any day now—all of this society BS will disappear. In that moment, we'll revert to the survival of the fittest. Kill or be killed.

Despite the pervasiveness of this story, it just isn't true. In the most extreme circumstances, people don't automatically revert to an animalistic Now Me. In moments of real crisis, we see bigger truths.

THIRTY-THREE ME'S

On August 5, 2010, hundreds of thousands of tons of rock suddenly collapsed deep underneath the ground of Chile's Atacama Desert.

Stuck beneath those piles of rock were thirty-three men. Miners hired to extract minerals and valuables from deep inside the Earth.

The miners were trapped. They lacked the ability to communicate with the outside world. No one above ground knew exactly where they were. The thirty-three men had enough food and water to feed ten men for only two days. It was a true Prisoner's Dilemma moment if there ever was one. So how Now Me did things get? Did the law of the jungle break out, with factions competing for meager resources and the strong killing the weak?

That's not what happened. The men didn't turn on each other. They organized.

It didn't happen immediately. The first day many of the men frantically looked for a way out. But after realizing their predicament, a few leaders stepped up. The men collaborated to create order, structure, and purpose. They assigned tasks. They decided how to ration resources by democratic vote. They simulated day and night by using electric lights. They encouraged each other when they became overwhelmed. They started each day with a prayer.

They weren't thirty-three Me's. They were an Us.

For more than two terrifying, unimaginable weeks without contact with the outside world, this is how these thirty-three men lived. They had no idea if they would ever be found, but they continued to live a structured and collaborative existence anyway. That's what it took to survive.

By the sixteenth day, food supplies had dwindled. The men were rationed down to one *bite* of food every three days. Still, they hung on.

And then, miraculously, on the seventeenth day a drill broke through a wall. They'd been found. Fifty-two days later all thirty-three men safely escaped the mine.

Had the miners approached their ordeal in a Now Me, Prisoner's Dilemma fashion, many if not all of these men would be dead. Every man for himself would have ended in disaster. The miners survived because they recognized the truth: they were going to live or die as one. By becoming an Us rather than thirty-three Me's, they found the way to live.

BENTOISM

Just because we're not trapped in a mine doesn't mean we're not stuck. We're stuck under the thumb of financial maximization. We're trapped by a limited perspective.

How do we become free of these limitations? By acknowledging how big the universe actually is.

It's not just this:

It's this:

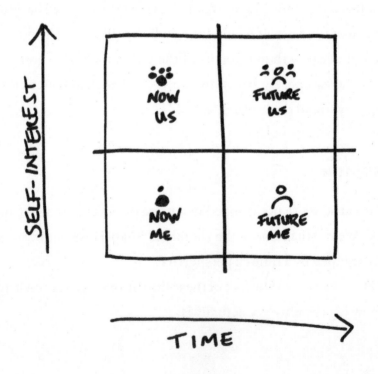

What would happen if this way of seeing value became normal? If considering the needs of Future Us and Now Us became common and accepted? Would more companies repair and encourage reuse of already existing products like Patagonia does? Would more car companies actively seek solutions to our environmental crises even if it harmed their near-term financial self-interest? Would CEOs willingly pay themselves less and pay workers more? Would we be able to satisfy our financial needs while also prioritizing the values that matter to us, like Adele?

Yes. Yes to these things and then some. Look at what humanity has created in pursuit of financial growth. Imagine what can be accomplished if we combine our capabilities with a broader understanding of value. A world where we aren't just focused on capturing value, we're focused on creating it. A world where we can all live more self-coherent lives.

How would that happen?

STEP 1: PERSONAL BENTOISM

Many of us can't say what our values are. We're too busy trying to achieve financial security (hoping it turns into becoming very well off financially) to search for a meaningful philosophy of life. Who has time for that?

How can we change that? How can we discover our own values?

It begins with a blank piece of paper.

That's how my Bento began. On that piece of paper, I drew a Bento box. Inside each box I wrote a question that got to the heart of what that Bento was about, and next to them I wrote each Bento's core values, too. The questions were straightforward: What do I want and need? What does my future self want and need? What do we want and need? What does future us want and need?

I gave myself five minutes to brainstorm responses to the questions. I tried not to overthink it. I wrote whatever came to mind. Here's what came out:

I spent more time looking for similarities and themes in what I'd written. What traits, values, or motivations did these ideas share? After some iteration, my Bento looked like this:

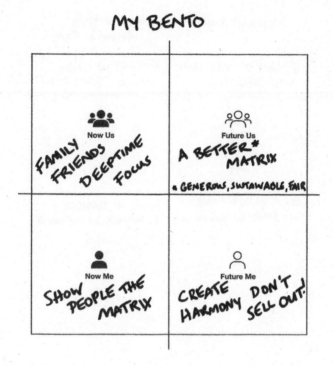

What am I motivated by? What's my purpose? My Bento shows me what these things are. These are my values. What drives me. The essence of who I am. Looking at this for the first time was affecting and revealing. These things felt true.

Once my Bento was set, I started asking it questions. I started off with day-to-day stuff. Here are some actual things I asked my Bento, and what it said.

Should I go on vacation with a friend's family?

FOCUSED DEEPTIME WITH FRIENDS	FUTURE US/NEW FAMILY TRADITION
Now Us	Future Us
YES	YES
MUST FINISH BOOK TOO MUCH WORK TO DO	KIND OF FAMILY HARMONY I LOVE MOST
Now Me	Future Me
NO	YES

Now Us, Future Us, and Future Me all said yes. The vacation would be with good friends, it would be quality time, and it kept alive a recent tradition of our families traveling together. The trip easily lined up with these Bentos.

Now Me, however, said no. I had a deadline for this book that I didn't want to miss. Though three Bentos said yes and one said no, we didn't take the vacation.

Let's do a harder one.

Part of how I earn a living is by public speaking. Organizations, schools, and events invite me to share my ideas with their audiences and pay me to do so. But sometimes I get invited to speak for a company whose work I'm not as comfortable with.

MY BENTO

Advertising agencies, financial services companies, or others that feel potentially off-values.

My instinct (and response) for these invitations is to decline them. It feels like selling out, so I don't do them. But then I asked the Bento this question.

Should I do a talk for a company I don't like?

DEEPTIME WITH IDEAS, CAN'T JUST PREACH TO CHOIR Now Us **YES**	TO BUILD A BETTER MATRIX YOU NEED THESE ORGS Future Us **YES**
SHOW PEOPLE THE MATRIX + SUPPORT YOURSELF Now Me **YES**	ARE YOU SURE YOU AREN'T SELLING OUT? Future Me **NO**

Now Me says do it. Giving a talk creates financial security and fulfills my purpose of showing people the matrix. My Bento doesn't say anything about who those people should be.

Now Us says do it. Am I meant to only preach to the choir? Maybe it's the places I'm most anxious about where my voice will most matter, and where I stand to learn the most.

Future Us says if the world is going to move away from financial maximization, it's these places that must evolve. I should view the chance to speak directly with those people as an opportunity and responsibility.

Future Me, however, still says no. It's concerned with the financial compensation that comes with this. It questions my intentions and tells me to watch my step. This is the voice that nagged me when I struggled with these decisions in the past. But now that I can put that voice in its Future Me context, I'm grateful it's there. It's like a bouncer looking out for my values. It's got my back.

Though I still sometimes decline speaking invitations for Future Me reasons, I'm more open than I used to be. Seeing it from a Bentoist perspective changed how I thought about this part of my life.

▪ ▪ ▪ ▪

With its more microscopic view on our values, the Bento exposes why some choices are harder for us than others. Think about one of the harder things people do: quit smoking. Let's imagine a smoker's Bento if they ask it whether they should quit.

Should a smoker quit smoking?

My family hates it, bad for my children **Now Us** YES	Imagine I'm the reason my kid starts smoking **Future Us** YES
I love smoking. Quitting will suck **Now Me** NO	Healthier longer life! **Future Me** YES

The smoker knows it's a bad thing to do. They know quitting is better for them long-term. They know it's better for their loved ones. And yet Now Me, with its pleasure-seeking, addictive tendencies, says it doesn't want to quit.

It's important to recognize that Now Me isn't being irrational. It's addicted to nicotine. The pain of quitting is hell. Who would choose to experience such a thing if they had the option? This is why our Now Me voice can be so stubborn: sometimes it has a valid point based on its limited—but rational—point of view. Just like financial maximization.

We tend to need outside help to change voices like these. There are positive and negative versions of this help, from encouragement by a partner to quit smoking to being scared straight after a bad doctor's visit. Being confronted by these voices can jolt someone onto a different path. But at the same time, the smoker already knows the reasons why they should quit. Still their Now Me voice says to keep smoking.

A more fruitful strategy would be to create a reality where a smoker's Now Me rationally says yes to quitting. How? By increasing the amount of effort it takes to smoke. And that's what society has effectively done. We've stigmatized cigarettes, made them expensive by putting high taxes on them, and banned smoking in public spaces to increase the amount of effort it takes to smoke. As the Now Us of society quits smoking—as it has done—more Now Me's quit, too. By prioritizing the values of the person who needs convincing, the chances of swaying someone's opinion or behavior are far greater.

■ ■ ■ ■

When I started using the Bento, I kept it pinned next to my desk and a picture of it on my phone. I found it useful to have a concrete reminder of my values in a world where magazines tell me to disrupt myself.

The Bento became second nature pretty quickly. Soon I could picture it in my mind, mentally ask it a question, and watch each Bento box flash red or green with a yes or no response. In family decisions, my wife and I started asking each other, "What does our Bento say?" and then talking through the perspectives. This helped clarify what was important, and what options were most in line with our values.

Sometimes a question required me to write down answers like you've seen. This gave me a more nuanced understanding of the situation. Maybe a Bento said no not because of the decision itself, but because of how I assumed it would happen. This allowed me to keep iterating on the situation until I arrived at a Y/Y/Y/Y result.

This doesn't mean that only Y/Y/Y/Y responses should be given a green light. As the earlier examples show, the responses I get from my Bento are often mixed. That's probably why I'm asking those particular questions in the first place. But even when I overrule what the Bento recommends, the increased awareness of my values has led to more self-coherent choices and a life more in accordance with my nature than I've lived before. It's taught me a new way to see.

Think this is impossible? It's not. Start with a blank piece of paper. You can do it, too.

STEP 2: ORGANIZATIONAL BENTOISM

A Bentoist sense of value in our personal lives is powerful. But it's not enough to counter financial maximization on its own. That's why we need organizations to align with a Bentoist value system, too.

Organizations—companies especially—wield enormous

influence. They're a driving force for financial maximization and the establishment of norms. If a mass shift to a Bentoist approach to value were to happen, companies would need to be partners leading the way.

This sounds like a hard sell. Why would companies willingly focus on more than just financial maximization? That seems antithetical to recent decades of trends.

This is true. But more than any other secular institution, organizations and companies have embraced the practice of using values to set expectations and guide decisions. There are questions about how sincere these values are (Enron naming "integrity" and "respect" as two of its core values, for example), but the validity of values as a way to shape decisions is more accepted in organizations than anywhere else.

And because of corporate structures like public benefit corporations, a company has the opportunity to give its values and beliefs legal standing that can last for generations. Companies are uniquely positioned to lead the future of how society thinks about values.

The Bento works for an organization just like it does for a person. The only difference is that an organization's "Me" refers to the self-interest of the organization itself, and the "Us" refers to employees, customers, community members, and others affected by what it does.

Here's a Bento I made for Apple, using what's public about the company's mission, identity, and strategy, as an example.

APPLE'S BENTO

Now Us WALLED GARDEN PRIVACY JUST WORKS	**Future Us** TOOLS + PLATFORMS THAT ADVANCE HUMANKIND
Now Me TOOLS THAT ADVANCE HUMANKIND	**Future Me** THINK DIFFERENT

This Bento (if it were based on the company's actual strategy, not my Canal Street knockoff) would serve as Apple's compass when making decisions. Which projects should we invest in? The ones most in line with our Bento. How should we make this new product? According to the Now Us values that our customers expect and the Future Me standards that we expect. And so on.

Once an organization identified its Bento values, its goals and metrics would evolve to reflect it. Financial targets would remain to ensure sustainability and profitability, but goals and metrics associated with Bentoist values would be elevated alongside them. The organization would shift from a singular focus on financial maximization to a dual focus on financial performance and creating value in whatever ways its mission called for.

This would bring every organization closer to the "spirit of coexistence and co-prosperity" that Konosuke Matsushita said companies and societies should share. "Every company, no matter how small, ought to have clear-cut goals apart from the pursuit of profit, purposes that justify its existence among us," he wrote. "Such goals are an avocation, a secular mission to the world."

For a company whose mission focuses on improving the health of the earth, the environmental impact of its products should be as serious a concern as the company's profitability. The company should be willing to give up some profitability—offering lifetime repairs like Patagonia does or "carbon-offset shipping" like the marketplace Etsy provides—in exchange for an investment in its mission-based values. It should be willing to use financial value to create non-financial value.

For secular missions to be real, they have to be as consequential as the company's financial concerns. If a company's leadership fails to take the company's environmental priorities seriously, the board must bring in new leaders who will. Creating accountability around these values makes clear that while this is a different way of doing business, it's still business. Results matter.

Other businesses may struggle to identify what values they truly support beyond vague platitudes that hang on cafeteria walls. Those businesses are in danger of irrelevance as the shift from old to new values accelerates. To hire quality people and earn a loyal clientele, businesses must do more than grow their bottom line. They must find their secular mission, the unique way they can create value for their communities. Businesses that create this kind of value will survive the shock waves of new business models and other disruptive changes, and last for the long haul. Those that don't, won't.

Expanding Bentoist values in partnership with organizations brings together the best of both worlds: the collaborative urgency of companies and the generative promise of value creation. This is the coprosperity that the world needs.

STEP 3: THE VALUES MAXIMIZING CLASS

It's 2050.

We're standing at the corner of Second Avenue and First Street in the Lower East Side. The same place where Mars Bar and TD Bank once stood. Both are long gone now. In their place today is an all-glass storefront, its doors open to the street.

Inside are rows of tables full of people. Some are older, some are young. Some are talking, others are staring intently into luminescent screens. A loop of graphs and other visualizations plays on the wall. Above the front door, a sign reads:

BENTO SOCIETY
Lower East Side Chapter

Beneath it a smaller, handwritten sign: "HSBChase Bank that way," with an arrow pointing outside to a set of stairs leading to the second floor.

Inside the Bento Society chapter, researchers for a recent set of community-growing experiments are sharing results. Four of their experiments failed to make a significant difference, but one showed promise. Others in the room riff on what that could mean.

Around the world, sixty of these meetings are happening that night. The monthly Bento Society meetings are where community members share insights and data from their experiments in growing nonfinancial values. There's no shame in sharing failed results. In such a new field, there's something to learn from everything.

■ ■ ■ ■

In 2050 a Bentoist view of value is a real thing. People better understand their values and live more self-coherent lives. Companies hold themselves accountable to a wider set of values that they take as seriously as their profitability. Slowly but surely over the course of thirty years, a belief in rational value beyond financial value becomes normal. A new hidden default.

As the Bentoist approach to value emerges, talented people become drawn to its unique challenges. Using your skills to maximize financial value seems like a waste when a whole new frontier of value awaits. Led by some of the best and brightest of the Millennial and Z generations, these people become the pioneers of the new Values Maximizing Class.

Accountants, carpenters, community organizers, construction workers, data scientists, designers, ecologists, economists, engineers, entrepreneurs, financial analysts, journalists, lawyers, line cooks, meteorologists, politicians, social scientists, teachers, truck drivers, venture capitalists, waitresses, students, and retirees dedicate themselves to the mission of identifying, measuring, and growing rational, nonfinancial values. Their work is funded and distributed by the Bento Society, whose Lower East Side chapter we just saw.

One of the group's first projects was to collect and analyze data from inside companies about their investments into values growth. After close examination of hundreds of case studies, researchers identified three primary paths to growing value:

1. Growing new value in new things
2. Growing new value in existing things
3. Growing existing value in existing things

The most successful project in the first path was the value-added credit (VAC), a government-backed, interest-bearing currency that rewards long-standing value-creating businesses and community centers. The VAC has helped thousands of neighborhood staples to remain and even expand as real estate prices have continued to rise.

But of the new-value-in-new-thing experiments, the VAC proves to be the only meaningful success. Others, like pop-up Values Spas and Values Bots, have good intentions but not much interest from the public.

Value-growing projects that follow the second and third paths—growing new or existing value in existing things—are a different story. Nearly every company surveyed had successfully grown the value of existing things. For example:

- Adele's experiment led to others reprogramming financially maximizing algorithms to maximize for fairness. This extended the value life of the original algorithms and allowed for fairness-maximizing strategies to be applied to housing, medical care, travel, and even traffic. These affirmative algorithms, as they were called, used the logic of reverse Dutch auctions to match price and competency minimums with need maximums in real estate, school access, and other uses of shared public resources.

- Companies reverse engineered the algorithms that cluster and rank their users for marketing purposes, and reused them to create mentorship and peer circles among community members. The segmenting tools helped group people in similar situations (people struggling with medical or financial challenges, people starting a business, new moms and dads) with others who were going through the same thing or had successfully navigated those waters before. This increased

the autonomy, community, knowledge, mastery, and purpose values of those individuals and platforms.

- To reduce resource use, many companies switched to the
  "evergreen" model, a subscription pricing approach to consumer goods. Customers pay a small amount up front and a
  monthly usage fee thereafter to continue owning the product ("evergreen" was initially a colloquial criticism because
  these products are forever costing money). Products come
  fully guaranteed with lifetime warranties and free repairs.
  Though controversial, evergreen products result in the production of fewer goods, consumption of fewer resources,
  and decreased consumerism, all while companies maintain
  and even increase profitability and employment in their mas-
  sive repair and reuse facilities.

The Values Maximizing Class's overview of this work—*Value
in the 21st Century*—proves significant. Among its most important
recommendations are standardizations of measurement for more
than a dozen nonfinancial values, and the formula for a new metric to track total value creation, called gross domestic value (GDV).

The establishment of standard measurements brings more
companies and even governments on board. Values growth is a new
infrastructure frontier. Nearly one out of five for-profit companies
adopt the dual purpose of profitability and mission-driven value
creation. A lot of it is hype, but a lot of it is also very real.

Wall Street analysts estimate that the market value of these companies is 20 percent less than their profit-only competitors. Analysis by the Bento Society, however, finds that once the nonfinancial values created by these companies are factored in, dual-purpose companies are significantly more value productive. Nonfinancial value is a good financial investment.

With people, organizations, institutions, and tools increasingly aligned behind this new sense of value, gross domestic value begins a hockey-stick rise in nations across the globe. Through an expansion of perspective, a world of scarcity becomes a world of abundance.

THE VALUES HELIX

For a future like this to occur, we all have a role to play. Not just our future selves. Us right now.

Each and every one of us is a conductor—and sometimes transformer—of a long chain of ideas and values from one end of time to the other. Which values continue and which values change is up to each of us.

The Bento shows how it works.

Here's a Bento, with each box slightly renamed to be more descriptive of what it represents.

Now Me is labeled Me.

Future Me is labeled Values. The things that are always true of you.

Now Us is labeled Relationships.

Future Us is named Me_2, meaning the next generation.

	Now Us		Future Us
	Relationships		Me_2
	Me		**Values**
	Now Me		Future Me

Here's my Bento. For me, Me_2 represents my son. Let's see what happens when we try building out his Bento.

Relationships	**Me₃**	
Now Us	*Future Us*	
Relationships	**Me₂**	**Values**
Me	**Values**	
Now Me	*Future Me*	

His Bento extends directly from mine. My Values and Relationships exert direct influence on him. My wife and I are the force pushing behind him, and our values are the foundation underneath him. He'll define and discover himself in life just like we all do, but we're a propulsive force behind and beneath him that forms who he is.

It's the same for Me₂ (my son) and Me₃ (his child, should he have one):

	Relationships	Me_4	
Relationships	Me_3	Values	
Now Us	Future Us		
Relationships	Me_2	Values	
Me	Values		
Now Me	Future Me		

Which also means that, going back a generation, the Me_{-1} values and relationships of my parents exerted the same influence on me. They set my baseline for how to value and view the world.

This chain keeps going. Values and norms keep passing from generation to generation. From one set of partygoers to the next. This is how the family way stays the family way. How a society stays continuous. I call the force that carries this the Values Helix.

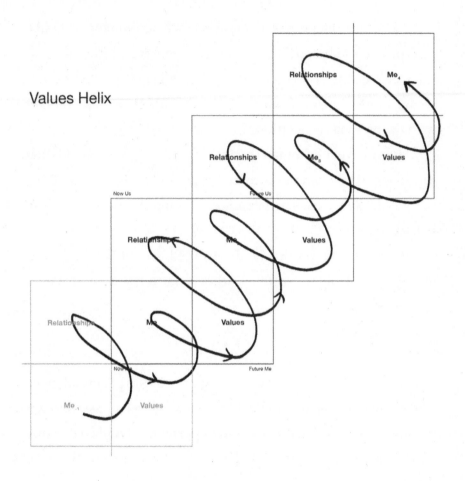

Values Helix

The Values Helix is a natural force propelled by time that carries our values, our customs, and even our hidden defaults across generations. The choices we collectively and individually make and the lives we live get swooped up by the Values Helix and directly affect the values of the generations that follow. The party doesn't stop.

The eighteenth-century Scottish philosopher David Hume tried imagining a world without generational influence.

To do this, he proposed a universe where humans lived like caterpillars and butterflies. The current generation (the caterpillar) would go into a cocoon and die. The next generation (the butterfly) would emerge from the cocoon without any interaction with the previous generation.

Hume gave this human the ability to redesign the world each time it emerged from the cocoon. What kind of world would this be? Would we make smarter choices? Would this be a better way to live?

It wasn't. The results, he determined, would be chaos. Too much would change too often. Without continuity, it would barely be a society at all.

■ ■ ■ ■

For all the challenges we face, we're equipped with profound tools. The collective wisdom and values that have been passed down by our ancestors' hard work and experience. The institutions built by previous generations. The technologies and skills we've developed.

To take advantage of these tools, we must live up to our responsibilities as humans. We must be conscious of the continuous process that keeps our cultures and values alive. We must be vigilant and aware of our role. Every single one of us has a part to play.

In areas where we want values to change, we should work to change them. They won't change on their own. But we also need to have the right expectations for how much effort change takes.

Just because we don't see the finish line in our lifetime doesn't mean we lost the race.

In areas where we want values to stay, we should use our energy to make sure they do. We should be vocal about the values that positively govern our families, communities, organizations, and lives. We should not take them for granted or leave them unsaid when debates of value come up.

Sometimes, despite our efforts, values that we love will diminish. In those moments we should be grateful for that same gradual process of change. We all need time to mourn what will pass and to adjust to the new normal.

■ ■ ■ ■

One day, in the not-too-distant future, financial maximization will be the value that's diminishing. The anomalies in the system will have added up. The crisis moment will have arrived.

What values will rise in its place? Will we expand our view of value? Will we learn to see self-interest in new ways? Will we shift from rational self-interest to rational self-coherence?

At the start of this book you may have said these are unrealistic goals. You still might. But I hope to have convinced you that an expanded understanding of value can greatly increase our potential. And that there's a whole world of value for each of us to unlock in our organizations and our lives.

There are many stops between here and there. The road is long. But it's like turning left. You just need a destination worth going to, and the determination to get there.

ACKNOWLEDGMENTS

This book was made possible by the generosity, support, and wisdom of so many people.

To my mom, Margie Sentelle, thank you for instilling in me a strong sense of values and a love for reading. I am very much your son. To my dad, C. G. Strickler, thank you for being a loving and sensitive father, and for giving me the gift of music. I love you so much. To my stepfather, Tommy Sentelle, and my stepmother, Karen Strickler, thank you both for decades of love and support. To my father-in-law, S. J. Kim, and my mother-in-law, Coco Kim, thank you for your love and care. To my brothers, Stephen Sentelle and Dylan Strickler, y'all aren't half bad, either.

To Perry Chen and Charles Adler, thank you for a lifetime-shaping partnership. This book wouldn't exist without the experiences we created and shared together. To everyone at Kickstarter past and present, thank you for your friendship, your dedication, for the ways you helped me grow as a person and a leader, and for being a beautiful family of humans.

My life as a writer wouldn't have happened without the encouragement of many mentors. This starts with my teachers: Ms. Johnson and Ms. Wontrop at Dayspring Christian Academy, Mr. Swope at Giles High School, and Sam Kashner and Varun Begley at the College of William & Mary. Thanks to each of you for investing in me and exposing me to new ideas. To my first editor, Madelyn Rosenberg, then of the *Roanoke Times* & *World-News*, thank you for humoring sixteen-year-old me. To Ryan Schreiber, thanks for taking a chance and inviting me to write for *Pitchfork* back in the day. To Ira Robbins, thank you for your mentorship and our friendship over the years. To Chuck Eddy, thanks for publishing the unsolicited record review I sent you in the *Village Voice*, and for letting me keep writing for you, too. To Michael Azerrad, thanks for making me your first hire at eMusic, and for writing *Come As You Are* and *Our Band Could Be Your Life*. To Fred Wilson, thanks for your mentorship as a board member, and for the clarity and honesty of your daily posts on *AVC*.

Thank you to all the people I got to collaborate with editorially over the years, including Joe Keyes, Alex Naidus, Jayson Greene, Michaelangelo Matos, Jocelyn Glei, Mark Mangan, Sascha Lewis, Anjuli Ayer, Nitsuh Abebe, Nick Sylvester, Willa Koerner, Cassie Marketos, Meaghan O'Connell, Mike McGregor, Brandon Stosuy, Brett Camper, Melissa Maerz, Rich Juzwiak, Joe Robinson, Michael Bryson, Spencer Kaufman, Chris Kaskie, Mark Richardson, Sean

Fennessey, Tom Ewing, Andy Kellman, David Carr, and Stanley Booth.

I was fortunate to be helped by many collaborators while writing this book.

To Julie Wood, thank you for challenging me to write the original Web Summit talk and for being a joyful human. To Laurel Schwulst, thanks for always being such a great collaborator, and for creating this future breath with me. To Tracy Ma, thanks for being an early collaborator on the art book version of this, and for making a helpful reference later on. To Miriam Garcia, thank you for your amazingly detailed research for this project. It mattered. To Evan Applegate, thanks for making the book's charts and for being so easy to work with. To Daniel Arnold, thanks for always being such a rad human and for taking my author photo on the morning of my fortieth birthday. To John Sundman, thanks for your fact-checking help and second pair of eyes on the book's thornier topics, and thanks to John Biggs for introducing us. To Zack Sears, thanks for riffing on cover designs. To James Miao, thank you for posting the talk on Hacker News and helping to spread early ideas. To Maris Kreizman and Shea Serrano, thank you for your book industry know-how and people recommendations. To Robin Sloan, thanks for recommending *Age of Fracture*, which ultimately led to Bentoism. To Katinka Barysch, thanks for your wisdom and for staring at me intently when the professor said the development of medicine redefined what it meant to be healthy. To Ken Tun, thanks for being my first backer—the book is on the way. To Iris Bohnet, thanks for letting me present an early version of the book in your classroom, and thanks to my YGL classmates for listening so generously. To Fred Benenson, thanks for checking my math. To Jason Kottke, thanks for recommending *Emperor of Maladies*, which informed the health section. To Christine Kantner, thanks for being a great friend and neighbor, and for inviting me to speak at your salon. To Waris Ahluwalia, thank you for your friendship and how generously you've helped put these ideas into the world. To Noel Osheroff, thank you for inviting me to write from your home. Our coworking relationship is a cherished memory.

A small handful of early readers were invaluable in keeping the book on the right path. To my friend Ian Hogarth, your brilliance and keen eyes for trends had as big an influence on the book as anyone. To my old friend Steve Eskay, thanks for giving honest feedback and for being so encouraging in moments of doubt. To Tristram Stuart and Simon Smiles, thanks for using your incredibly valuable time to help make this book better. To my friends Elisabeth Holm, Jason Butler, Rafael Rozendaal, Haden Polseno-Hensley, and Justin Kazmark, thanks for reading early drafts. To Alex Taborrak, thanks for being willing to share not just what you loved, but what you hated about the book. To my friends Adam Curtis, Ian Rogers, and Simon Russell, thanks for lending an ear and your brains to these ideas.

To Michael Walzer, the philosopher who wrote *Spheres of Justice*, and Elizabeth Anderson, the philosopher who wrote *Value in Ethics and Economics*, thank you for your brilliant ideas. I hope this book takes them a significant step forward into the public consciousness. To Robert Gibbs, thank you for humoring my questions about the no-left-turn rule. To Jonathan Bowles, thanks for sharing your nuanced understanding of New York City, and for all the work you've done to help the city over the years (and thanks to Eli Dvorkin for introducing us). To Kohei Nishida, thank you for buying many bentos and for taking the official bento photograph. To Tim Rohan and Stan Connors, thanks for allowing me to use the mullet photo (and congrats on a truly amazing one, Stan). To Adam Grant, thank you for the incredible generosity of your advice and time. Thank you to all the amazing writers who agreed to read the book and share kind words, and for what I've learned from their own books. Thanks to the musicians Erlend Øye, Solange, Hailu Mergia, Pharoah Sanders, Alice Coltrane, Mulatu Astaske, Frank Ocean, Durutti Column, Future, Kurt Vile, J Dilla, and Eugene McDaniels, whose music inspired me and kept me company while my brain spun. Thanks to the Ideaspace for speaking to me throughout this process, and to Alan Moore for articulating the Ideaspace's existence, and to John Higgs for writing so brilliantly about it in his book about the KLF.

Thank you to the rest of my New York family, including Kendel and Adam Shore, Bridget and Charles Best, Laurence Carty and Paola Antonelli, Lena Iwamura, Agnieszka Kurant, Michal Rosen, Anthony Volodkin, Josh Stylman, Peter Hershberg, Alan Del Rio Ortiz, CJ Anderson, Pete Fritz, Ed Coleman, Greg Costello, Maureen Hoban, Jamin Warren, Jess Phelps, Jesse Ball, Qanta Shimizu, Doug Sherrard, and Liz Cook. Also thanks to Jerry Colonna, Chad Dickerson, Patrick Collison, Ev Williams, Andy Baio, Sunny Bates,

Tina Roth Eisenberg, Lance Ivy, Hope Hall, Jeff Hammerbacher, Tim O'Reilly, Jess Search, Jennifer Pahlka, Joi Ito, Karin Chien, Keri Putnam, Luis Von Ahn, Max Temkin, Deray McKeesson, Lawrence Lessig, Daryl Morey, Tyler Cowen, and Thaniya Keerepart. To my Echo Park family, Trish and Tony Unruh, Lucien Unruh, Rohan Ali, Alexa Meade, Anna Bulbrook, and Sadye Henson, thank you for making us feel so at home. To the 29 Palms Inn, thank you for always being a place of inspiration and solace. To New York City, the Lower East Side, and Chinatown, this book would have never happened without your energy and inspiration. Over two decades, you gave me so much.

To my agent, Daniel Greenberg, thanks for believing in me and being skeptical of me at the same time. Your high standards set an early bar for me to work toward. To my editor, Emily Wunderlich, thank you for taking a chance on me, for guiding this book thoughtfully and gently, for always knowing the right way to pose a hard question, for making sure this book could be all that it could be, and for always believing in me. I'm so lucky the universe brought us together.

Finally, and most importantly, I want to thank my spectacular wife, Jamie Kim, and son, Koji. The two of you are the light of my life, my daily inspiration, my absolute everything. Jamie, throughout this long and challenging process you were patient, always willing to listen, always there to encourage and tell me that I could do it, and always ready with words of wisdom. Your love means everything. I love you so much. And Koji, you are my son and my hero. I look at you now, only three years old, and see a sensitive, caring, and brilliant boy that takes my breath away. It's only been three years and I feel like I'm already running out of things to teach you. I can't wait for the day you're old enough to read this book and find your place in the world. I'm already so proud of whatever you will do.

This list, as long as it is, leaves out so many people who have meant so much. I'm unbelievably fortunate that so many amazing people have made a difference in my life. To all of them, thank you. And thanks to you, reader, for giving this book your time and attention. I know how precious those things are.

Peace and love,
Yancey

APPENDIX

This section is the liner notes I wish existed for every book I've loved. It includes a deeper look at the philosophical roots of Bentoism, a suggested reading list, expanded thoughts on the thirty-year theory of change, and more.

THE ORIGINS OF BENTOISM

I've long held a belief that our notion of value was too narrow. I remember reading a piece in *Harper's Magazine* more than a decade ago (which I've been unable to track down) about how GDP failed to classify whether money was spent in a socially positive or negative way. This idea stayed with me. How could our measurement systems be so broad and blunt?

While cofounding and leading Kickstarter, these instincts became stronger. We were clear on money's importance: we wanted to be independent, we wanted autonomy, and this meant we needed to operate in the black. But we were also clear about how money could become problematic. How a desire to constantly grow and enrich oneself leads to near-term thinking and abandonment of values.

At the encouragement of a colleague at Kickstarter, Julie Wood, I spoke about financial maximization at Web Summit, as mentioned in the book. I continued to touch on the subject in every talk I gave as CEO thereafter.

In 2017 I stepped down as Kickstarter's CEO and began thinking more about the role of financial value versus other values. What was the history of our belief in financial value? Why were we so sure that money was what mattered? What was the justification for this belief? This led me into a rabbit hole of research and reading, some of which informs the first half of this book.

In my reading I encountered much on the history of money, the importance of money, and the evils of money. But I struggled to find explorations of the value space beyond money the way that I was thinking about it. I wanted to make the case that nonfinancial value was just as rational as financial value. Had anyone made this case before?

And then one day I found something. While reading a fascinating book called *Age of Fracture* by Daniel Rodgers, I came across mention of a movement called communitarianism, where a more expansive set of values was embraced. In fact, one of the core game theorists at the RAND Corporation (John Nash, subject of the biography and film *A Beautiful Mind*) moved to a communitarian community in the 1970s. Intrigued, I continued to dig into communitarianism until I came across a book by Michael Walzer.

Walzer is a professor emeritus of social science at Princeton University's Institute for Advanced Study. He wrote *Spheres of Justice: A Defense of Pluralism and Equality* in 1983. It was in this little-known book that I discovered a different notion of value.

Our problem, as Walzer sees it, is dominance. Money—and other values of the past—dominates in spheres beyond where it rightfully should. "Birth and blood, landed wealth, capital, education, divine grace, and state power have all served to dominate or enable some group to dominate others," he observes.

As a result, we fail to reach ideal outcomes in many areas of life. The potential of our world is unjustly compromised by the domination of others. Walzer notes the seventeenth-century French polymath Blaise Pascal's writings on tyranny in his 1670 collection *Pensées*.

"The nature of tyranny is to desire power over the whole world and outside its own sphere . . . [it's] the desire of universal power beyond its scope."

Pascal goes on:

There are different companies—the strong, the handsome, the intelligent, the devout—and each man reigns in his own, not elsewhere. But sometimes they meet, and the strong and the handsome fight for mastery—foolishly, for their mastery is of different kinds. They misunderstand one another, and make the mistake of each aiming at universal dominion. Nothing can win this, not even strength, for it is powerless in the kingdom of the wise.

We are a world of many masters, not just one. Each domain has its rightful ruling values and ways of valuing.

Walzer's proposal is to limit the impact of money or any other dominant value through something he alternately calls "complex equality" and "political egalitarianism." The aim of this is "a society free from domination."

Walzer's counterintuitive insight is that just dominance within a sphere is fine. Justice should be dominant in areas relating to justice. Love should be dominant in areas of the heart. Each value has its own rightful place where it should rule. According to Walzer, even a business monopoly within a category can be fine. These monopolies and dominant positions can be justly earned and to everyone's benefit.

The problem is when they rule where they shouldn't. "We should focus on the reduction of dominance, not or not primarily the breakup or constraint of monopoly," Walzer writes. "Consider what it would mean to narrow the range within which goods are convertible to other spheres." He continues:

Imagine now a society in which different social goods are monopolistically held—as they are in fact and always will be, barring continual state intervention—but in which no particular good is vernally convertible . . . The resistance to convertibility would be maintained, in large degree, by ordinary men and women within their own spheres of competence and control, without large-scale state action.

This is a little opaque, but he's asking us to consider a society where each sphere has its own rules and criteria. Just because you have a lot of money doesn't mean you get to be beautiful. Beauty is a whole different category. You don't get one because you have the other. And this is something that people can control on their own through their values and how they hold on to them.

We each have our areas in which we excel; however, this shouldn't give us undue rights in areas where our talents and merits do not deserve it. Walzer writes:

Citizen X may be chosen over citizen Y for political office, then the two of them will be unequal in the sphere of politics. But they will not be unequal generally so long as X's office gives him no advantages over Y in any other sphere—superior medical care, access to better schools for his children, entrepreneurial opportunities, and so on.

Financial inequality wouldn't matter as much if money was not so dominant. Having a lot of money would be like having a lot of toilet paper. Good for one purpose but not for everything.

It just doesn't matter, from the standpoint of complex equality, that you have a yacht and I don't, or that the sound system of her hi-fi set is greatly superior to his. People will focus on such matters or not: that is a question of culture, not justice. So long as yachts and hi-fi sets and rugs have only use value and individualized symbolic value, their unequal distribution does not matter.

Walzer's vision is a world without dominance. A world where each sphere of life is ruled by its own values, not dominated by others. Because, as Walzer writes, "We are all culture-producing creatures whose customs have meaning and any attempts to override them are tyrannical."

The answer isn't one idea or way flourishing, it's all ideas and ways flourishing:

We can imagine society being run by a hereditary king, a benevolent despot, a landed aristocracy, a capitalist executive committee, a regime of bureaucrats, or a revolutionary vanguard. The argument for democracy is that different companies of men and women will most likely be respected if all the members of all the companies share political power.

We find this hard to accept because of the myths of Great Men that we've been fed. Walzer again:

We are told stories about the war hero turned entrepreneur turned perfect orator. These stories are fictions, the conversion of money or power or academic talent into legendary fame. Even if they do exist, there aren't enough of these people to create a ruling class. By and large the most accomplished politicians, entrepreneurs, scientists, soldiers, and lovers will be different people. So long as the goods they possess don't bring other goods in train, we have no reason to fear their accomplishments.

Reading Walzer opened my mind. I kept thinking about the notion of each value having a rightful domain. If this is true, how do we know what domain we're in? How can we know the values at stake?

A year later I came across a second book that transformed my thinking: a 1993 book called *Value in Ethics and Economics* by philosopher Elizabeth Anderson. Anderson, a professor at the University of Michigan, hones in on, and builds upon, Walzer's idea of a pluralistic notion of value. She writes:

We don't respond to what we value merely with desire or pleasure, but with love, admiration, honor, respect, affection, and awe as well. This allows us to see how goods can be plural, how they can differ in kind or quality: they differ not only in *how much* we should value them, but in *how* we should value them . . . The variety of ways of caring about things is the source of pluralism in my theory of value.

In contrast, Anderson says our money-driven way of doing things convinces us "that we care about things that aren't really important, justify our actions on things we don't really believe in. And that to do this will create material wealth. So what if it doesn't fit your character. That's just the price we pay. It fails to provide us with a coherent basis for self-understanding and requires disturbing divisions among different aspects of the self."

She goes on:

There is a great diversity of worthwhile ideals, not all of which can be combined in a single life. Different ideals may require the cultivation of incompatible virtues or the pursuit of some projects that necessarily preclude the pursuit of others. Individuals with different talents, temperaments, interests, opportunities, and relations to others rationally adopt or uphold different ideals. Since ideals direct a person to specially value some worthwhile projects, persons, and things over others, they distinguish from among all goods those that are particularly important to the individual. That incompatible ideals are properly adopted by different persons explains why it doesn't make sense for everyone to take up the same attitudes toward the same things. There are far more potentially worthy objects of valuation than could occupy any one person's concern.

In her embrace of a pluralistic view on value, which Anderson calls "expressive value," she introduces a new critical step:

Rather than determining which option will maximize your ideal outcome, this approach says the first step is to see what frame this fits in and to see what the right expressive norms and practical responses should be.

By taking this step, we can create more alignment between our values and ourselves.

"Expressive theories provide a coherent basis for self-understanding, accounting for the unity of the self, and making sense of ordinary intuitions about intrinsic value and norms of appropriate behavior and feeling," she writes.

We make decisions based on who and where we are, and what the norms around us suggest are the right and wrong ways of acting. And this is generally a good thing. This is how communities and people are distinct and how people are able to live in a self-cohesive way. It's this energy—subtle and deep—that financial maximization has overwhelmed.

Walzer's and Anderson's ideas kept turning over in my head. Then one day I was sketching on paper when I had my eureka moment: drawing a hockey stick graph, and seeing the great uncharted territory of self-interest that lay beyond. I thought about that other space that I'd never considered before. I extended the axes of the chart and drew dotted lines to delineate four quadrants, exactly as I do in the book.

Next to the sketch I scribbled a description of what I'd drawn. "*Beyond near-term orientation,*" I wrote. That's what the chart did. It took us beyond our near-term orientation.

I looked at it again. BEyond Near-Term Orientation.

BENTO. The picture was a bento box.

For more on Bentoism, including a guided process for building your own Bento, visit: **https://www.ystrickler.com/bento**

FURTHER READING

The following books were influences on this text and are recommended.

Bentoism

Elizabeth Anderson, *Value in Ethics and Economics*
Michael Walzer, *Spheres of Justice: A Defense of Pluralism and Equality*

How Ideas Work

Yuval Noah Harari, *Sapiens: A Brief History of Humankind*
John Higgs, *The KLF: Chaos, Magic, and the Band Who Burned a Million Pounds*
John Higgs, *Stranger Than We Can Imagine: An Alternative History of the 20th Century*
Thomas Kuhn, *The Structure of Scientific Revolutions*
Daniel Rodgers, *Age of Fracture*
J. Z. Young, *Doubt and Certainty in Science: A Biologist's Reflections on the Brain*

Economics

Rutger Bregman, *Utopia for Realists: How We Can Build the Ideal World*
David Graeber, *Debt: The First 5,000 Years (Updated and Expanded)*
Annie Lowrey, *Give People Money: How a Universal Basic Income Would End Poverty, Revolutionize Work, and Remake the World*
Mariana Mazzucato, *The Entrepreneurial State: Debunking Public vs. Private Sector Myths*

Mariana Mazzucato, *The Value of Everything: Making and Taking in the Global Economy*

Carlota Perez, *Technological Revolutions and Financial Capital: The Dynamics of Bubbles and Golden Ages*

Thomas Picketty, *Capital in the Twenty-First Century*

E. F. Schumacher, *Small Is Beautiful: Economics as If People Mattered*

Joseph Stiglitz, Amartya Sen, and Jean-Paul Fitoussi, *Mismeasuring Our Lives: Why GDP Doesn't Add Up*

Business

Yvon Chouinard, *Let My People Go Surfing: The Education of a Reluctant Businessman*

Phil Knight, *Shoe Dog: A Memoir by the Creator of Nike*

Michael Lewis, *Liar's Poker*

Konosuke Matsushita, *Not for Bread Alone*

Daniel H. Pink, *Drive: The Surprising Truth About What Motivates Us*

Financial Independence Retire Early

Chris Martenson and Adam Taggart, *Prosper! How to Prepare for the Future and Create a World Worth Inheriting*

Medicine

Siddhartha Mukherjee, *The Emperor of All Maladies: A Biography of Cancer*

David Wootton, *Bad Medicine: Doctors Doing Harm Since Hippocrates*

FURTHER WATCHING

The Adam Curtis films *The Trap*, *The Century of Self*, and *Hyper-Normalisation*

INTRODUCTION

ix **front page of *China Daily*:** The *China Daily* headline ran on October 27, 2017.

xiii **a healthy society:** Tucker Carlson's monologue was delivered on January 3, 2019, on Fox News.

xiv **poll by Harvard's Institute of Politics:** Harvard's Institute of Politics poll about young people and capitalism was reported in *Time* magazine ("American Capitalism's Great Crisis," May 11, 2014).

CHAPTER ONE: A SIMPLE IDEA

6 **based on Kickstarter:** Before Kickstarter launched, the musicians Marillion and Jill Sobule, as well as the platforms ArtistShare, DonorsChoose, Fundable, Indiegogo, and Sellaband, had done crowdfunding or something like it.

8 **"It seemed like the thing to do":** The story of the high five comes from *ESPN The Magazine* ("History of the High Five," August 8, 2011).

9 **they could, too:** My Web Summit talk is on YouTube under the title "Resist and Thrive—Yancey Strickler, Co-Founder of Kickstarter."

10 **The term "crowdfunding":** "Crowdfunding" was coined by journalist Jeff Howe in 2006. Kickstarter never embraced the phrase, but it seems here to stay.

12 **product and terms:** The "Why Kickstarter?" blog post went up on April 29, 2009.

13 **he wanted to buy the first copy:** The man from Myanmar who gave me the first $20 was Ken Tun. Thanks, Ken!

14 **10 billion people by 2050:** Population projections come from the UN's World Population Prospects report.

15 **his final user experience:** Steve Jobs's last words were reported by his sister, Mona Simpson ("A Sister's Eulogy for Steve Jobs," *New York Times*, October 30, 2011).

15 **ten years old in our species' life span:** Will MacAskill's perspective on the age of humanity comes from a 2018 TED Talk called "What Are the Most Important Moral Problems of Our Time?" MacAskill is also cofounder of a movement called effective altruism, which seeks to maximize the altruistic impact people create in their lives.

CHAPTER TWO: THE NO-LEFT-TURN RULE

18 **the world of retail planning:** I came across the "no-left-turn rule" after reading about Robert Gibbs, an urban retail planner, in a 1994 article in *The Atlantic*. Gibbs told the reporter that "the traffic advisor is the one that has all the sway . . . He vetoed so many sites that he was called The Terminator." Gibbs also wrote about this in his 2012 book *Principles of Urban Retail Planning and Development*. Bob Gibbs was kind enough to speak with me. I asked whether the no-left-turn rule was still alive and well. He assured

me that it continues to guide where shopping centers and stores are built today.

19 **Cass Sunstein has written:** Cass Sunstein wrote about white lines in parking lots as a kind of hidden default in his 2008 book with Richard Thaler, *Nudge.*

20 **citizens are default opted-out:** Data on organ donation rates comes from a 2004 study, "Defaults and Donation Decisions," by Eric J. Johnson and Daniel G. Goldstein.

20 **keep paying anyway:** Data on gym attendance rates comes from *USA Today* ("Is Your Gym Membership a Good Investment?," April 27, 2016).

20 **keep getting spammed:** Data on email unsubscribe rates comes from the email services provider MailChimp ("Email Marketing Benchmarks," March 2018, https://mailchimp.com/resources/email-marketing-benchmarks).

21 **approval rate layered on top:** Data on congressional approval ratings and reelection rates comes from the Center for Responsive Politics.

22 **"What's water?":** The David Foster Wallace story is paraphrased from a commencement address he gave at Kenyon College called "This Is Water."

22 **shift our behavior:** Daniel Kahneman and Amos Tversky's work is collected in the book *Thinking, Fast and Slow.*

22 **how we think:** Dan Ariely writes about our emotions' effect on our choices in his 2008 book *Predictably Irrational: The Hidden Forces That Shape Our Decisions.*

23 **62 percent of personal bankruptcies:** 62 percent of American bankruptcies are caused by medical bills according to a 2009 report published in the *American Journal of Medicine* ("Medical Bankruptcy in the United States, 2007: Results of a National Study" by David U. Himmelstein, Deborah Thorne, Elizabeth Warren, and Steffie Woolhandler).

23 **reap growing profits:** Examples of companies raising drug prices of existing drugs include the EpiPen, insulin (by three major manufacturers), and Daraprim.

23 **not workers or the future:** Data on more money spent on buy-backs than R&D in 2018 comes from a CNBC report ("Capital Expenditures Surge to 25-Year High, R&D Jumps 14% as Companies Spend Tax Cut Riches Freely," September 17, 2018).

29 **model of rational behavior:** As found in *The Compleat Strategyst: Being a Primer on the Theory of Games of Strategy* by J. D. Williams (page 23).

30 **ideal outcome of the game:** The story of the RAND Corporation secretaries is taken from Douglas Rushkoff's *Life Inc.: How Corporatism Conquered the World, and How We Can Take It Back,* and Adam Curtis's BBC documentary *The Trap.*

30 **rational thing to do:** Game theory wasn't literally suggesting people should turn their friends into the police. These strategies were rational *when playing within the parameters of the game.* The problems came when others began acting like the real world was one of these games.

33 **how important these cues about how to play really are:** The study on the power of naming in the Wall Street Game versus the Community Game comes from a paper by Varda Liberman, Steven M. Samuels, and Lee Ross called "The Name of the Game: Predictive Power of Reputations versus Situational Labels in Determining Prisoner's Dilemma Game Moves."

CHAPTER THREE: WHY EVERYTHING IS THE SAME

37 **Hot Country Songs chart:** I learned of the phenomenon of Sam Hunt's "Body Like a Back Road" through an email by journalist Jesse Rifkin published on the blog Marginal Revolution on September 22, 2017 (https://marginalrevolution.com/marginalrevolution/2017/09/slower-turnover-songs-movies.html).

39 **"broadcaster's judgment":** From a paper by Rachel M. Stilwell called "Which Public—Whose Interest—How the FCC's Deregulation of Radio Station Ownership Has Harmed the Public Interest, and How We Can Escape from the Swamp," published in 2006 in the *Loyola of Los Angeles Entertainment Law Review* (page 385).

39 **ten years before:** The story of radio's changeover came from multiple sources, including the *Los Angeles Times* ("Clear Channel's Dominance Obscures Promotions Conduit," by Jeff Leeds in 2001); a 2006 report by the nonprofit Future of Music Coalition entitled "False Premises, False Promises: A Quantitative History of Ownership Consolidation in the Radio Industry"; the previously mentioned paper by Rachel M. Stilwell, "Which Public— Whose Interest—How the FCC's Deregulation of Radio Station Ownership Has Harmed the Public Interest, and How We Can Escape from the Swamp"; and reporting by *Monterey County Now* ("In an Era of Consolidation, the Future of Radio Is Uncertain," September 1, 2016).

40 **songs they played:** According to "False Premises, False Promises: A Quantitative History of Ownership Consolidation in the Radio Industry," a 2006 paper by Peter DiCola of the Future of Music Coalition.

41 **box office top ten each year since 1950:** Data for the number of sequels, prequels, reboots, and remakes to be in the box office top ten comes from analysis by researcher Miriam Garcia for this book.

42 **remakes, sequels, or adaptations:** This statistic comes from the film data researcher Stephen Follows in a June 8, 2015, blog post entitled "How Original Are Hollywood Movies?" (https://stephen follows.com/how-original-are-hollywood-movies).

42 **significant stakes in movie studios:** Background on film and corporate consolidation comes from research by film historian Tim Dirks in "The History of Film: The 1980s" (https://www.filmsite .org/80sintro.html).

42 **expert told ABC:** The quote about the safety of making sequels is from Anita Busch, film editor for *Deadline,* speaking to *ABC News* ("What's Driving the Resurgence of Reboots, Remakes, and Revivals in TV and Film," May 2017).

43 **diversity of ideas decreased:** Background on the history of movie sequels comes from Stuart Henderson, author of *The Hollywood Sequel: History and Form, 1911–2010.*

44 **461 more than a decade before:** Data about the growth of bank branches comes from the *Wall Street Journal* ("All Those Banks in New York City? It's Our Fault," June 6, 2014).

45 **were not welcome:** As quoted in Hank's 2015 *New York Times* obituary, from a comment he made to a *New York Observer* reporter in 2005.

45 **$3,500 a month:** Data on the history of New York City rents comes from research by New York City real estate appraiser Jonathan Miller published in a New York real estate company magazine ("Change Is the Constant in a Century of New York City Real Estate," *Elliman* magazine) and reported in the *New York Times* ("In an Earlier Time of Boom and Bust, Rentals Also Gained Favor," October 17, 2011).

46 **$21,000 a month:** The story of a laundromat's rent going from $7,000 to $21,000 comes from *Harper's Magazine* ("The Death of a Once Great City," July 2018).

47 **bank branches in Manhattan alone:** All statistics in this paragraph come from the Center for an Urban Future's 2017 State of the Chains report.

47 **man who invented the boxer-brief:** John Varvatos is the inventor of the boxer-brief and owner of the upscale fashion store that's now in the former CBGB.

47 **chain stores in all of New York:** Information on the rise of chains in New York comes from the State of the Chains study commissioned annually by the nonprofit Center for an Urban Future since 2008. The statistic that the Lower East Side had the most chain stores (tied with Koreatown) comes from the 2017 State of the Chains report. I spoke with the Center for an Urban Future's director, Jonathan Bowles, whose characterizations of the changes to the city informed portions of this text. Though not a direct source, Jeremiah Moss's *Vanishing New York* blog and book are also powerful overviews of what's happened to New York City.

49 **"accelerated depreciation":** Information on the rise of the mall and the history of tax depreciation comes from historian Thomas Hanchett's paper "U.S. Tax Policy and the Shopping-Center Boom of the 1950s and 1960s," published by the American Historical

Association in 1996. I came across this paper after a Malcolm Gladwell *New Yorker* article on the history of the mall ("The Terrazzo Jungle," March 15, 2004) referenced it.

49 a **"permanent postponement of taxes"**: Federal Reserve economist William Hellmuth Jr.'s 1955 paper "Depreciation and the 1954 Internal Revenue Code" said that the tax code change amounted to a "permanent postponement of taxes."

50 **1961 *Wall Street Journal***: "Profits in Losses," *Wall Street Journal*, July 17, 1961.

51 **dropped by 77 percent**: Data on the decline of retail activity in city centers comes from Robert Gibbs's previously mentioned book, *Principles of Urban Retail Planning and Development*. The book notes, "In a single generation, the shopping mall remade more than 400 years of American city building." It also notes, "To a large degree, form follows rent."

51 **from existing local businesses**: According to the 1996 paper "What Happened When Wal-Mart Came to Town? A Report on Three Iowa Communities with a Statistical Analysis of Seven Iowa Counties," by Thomas Muller and Elizabeth Humstone for the National Trust for Historic Preservation.

51 **twelve thousand other stores**: From a paper by the Center for Economic Studies titled "The Evolution of National Retail Chains: How We Got Here," published in 2015. This paper also provided background on the growth, scale, and operations of chains.

51 **back to the local community**: According to Civic Economics' Andersonville Study of Retail Economics (2004), $68 of every $100 spent at a local retailer was redistributed locally versus $43 for a chain.

52 **used to be entrepreneurs, too**: This comes from the Kauffman Foundation's "Kauffman Index," which surveys rates of entrepreneurship in the United States. These particular data points come from its "Startup Density" index. Statistics on the decline of smoking rates come from Gallup's annual survey about smoking habits since the 1940s. In 1977, 38 percent of Americans told Gallup that they smoked. In 2015, 19 percent of Americans did.

52 **starting a business:** According to the 2018 UPS Stores' Inside Small Business Survey as reported by USA Today ("Survey: Two-thirds of Americans Dream of Opening a Small Business," May 4, 2018).

53 **keeps moving higher:** Information on the growth of chains comes from a paper called "Supersize It: The Growth of Retail Chains and the Rise of the 'Big Box' Retail Format" by two officials from the Census Bureau, based on forty years of census data on the size and expansion of businesses. Published in the *Journal of Economics and Management Strategy* in 2012, the paper notes that "until the late 1970s, more than half of all of the consumer dollars were spent at single-store retailers; [in 2012] more than 60% of consumer dollars are spent at a chain store, double the share of 1954." The same Census officials wrote another paper used as a source, called "The Evolution of National Retail Chains: How We Got Here," for the Census Bureau's Center for Economic Studies.

53 **entrepreneurship rates are declining:** News of decreasing tech start-up rates was reported in a National Bureau of Economic Research paper, "Changing Business Dynamism and Productivity: Shocks vs Responsiveness," by Ryan Decker, John Haltiwanger, Ron Jarmin, and Javier Miranda in 2018.

55 **malls in America will be closed:** According to a 2018 report by Credit Suisse ("Traditional Stores Are Doomed," April 18, 2018).

55 **"watching the *Titanic* sink":** From *Time* magazine ("Why the Death of Malls Is About More Than Shopping," July 20, 2017).

CHAPTER FOUR: THE MULLET ECONOMY

57 **solid waste was recycled:** Data on recycling rates comes from the most recent Environmental Protection Agency fact sheet from 2015.

58 **too dirty or isn't recyclable:** Data on the switch from multistream to single-stream recycling comes from *Scientific American* ("Single Stream Recycling," September 2013). More information came from *Wired* ("Listen Up America: You Need to Learn How to Recycle. Again," August 21, 2015).

58 **"made into another product"**: According to the Container Recycling Institute ("Understanding Economic and Environmental Impacts of Single-Stream Collection Systems," 2009).

59 **China was discarded**: Information on China's new rules for recycling comes from the *Wall Street Journal* ("Amid Trade Feud, Recycling Is in Danger of Landing on Trash Pile," April 12, 2018).

59 **what else to do**: Reports that waste facilities outside of Philadelphia were suspected of burning their recycling came from the *Guardian* ("'Moment of Reckoning': US Cities Burn Recyclables after China Bans Imports," February 2019).

59 **"our own worst enemies"**: As reported in the *Wall Street Journal* ("Recycling, Once Embraced by Businesses and Environmentalists, Now Under Siege," May 13, 2018)

60 **the case for financial maximization**: Milton Friedman's *New York Times* essay was titled "The Social Responsibility of Business Is to Increase Its Profits," published on September 13, 1970.

61 **single goal: to maximize profitability**: Background on what I call the Maximizing Class comes from several sources. Most important is analysis by economists William Lazonick and Mary O'Sullivan. In a paper called "Maximizing Shareholder Value: A New Ideology for Corporate Governance," published in the journal *Economy and Society* in 2010, Lazonick and O'Sullivan detail the history of what I call financial maximization. Their research finds that before the early 1970s when this new idea emerged, companies followed a "retain and reinvest" model, where profits were turned into additional services, products, pay raises, and training for employees. Starting in the 1970s, however, companies shifted to a strategy called "downsize and divest," where the strategy changed to smaller workforces and larger executive and shareholder bonuses. The practices they describe are the actions I attribute to the Maximizing Class.

62 **"in modern history"**: This comes from *The Firm: The Story of McKinsey and Its Secret Influence on American Business* by Duff McDonald.

64 **grew just 9.2 percent**: Data for historic pay rates comes from "The Productivity-Pay Gap," an Economic Policy Institute

analysis published in 2018 based on data from the Bureau of Labor Statistics.

64 **27 percent between 1979 and 2016:** According to a research report by the Economic Policy Institute, titled "CEO Compensation Surged in 2017."

65 **see what's happened:** Data on outstanding credit in America comes from the "Federal Reserve's Consumer Credit Outstanding (Levels) 1943–2018" and the US Census Bureau's Households by Type data.

67 **tends to go up:** Background on stock buybacks comes from economist William Lazonick's 2010 Brookings Institution paper "Stock Buybacks: From Retain-and-Reinvest to Downsize-and-Distribute," and his 2011 paper "From Innovation to Financialization: How Shareholder Value Ideology Is Destroying the US Economy" (published in the Oxford University Press collection *The Handbook of the Political Economy of Financial Crises*). Additional background came from "Stock Buybacks: Misunderstood, Misanalyzed, and Misdiagnosed" by Aswath Damodaran for the American Association of Individual Investors, and data from a research report by Goldman Sachs analyst Stuart Kaiser.

68 **"investors as a whole":** The *Fortune* article that initially highlighted buybacks was titled "Beating the Market by Buying Back Stock," by Carol J. Loomis on April 29, 1985.

70 **spent on stock buybacks:** Data on money spent on buybacks versus other investments comes from Deloitte ("Decoding Corporate Share Buybacks: Is It at the Cost of Investment?" November 2017).

71 **"footprint and influence":** *Financial Times* ("China Is Winning the Global Tech Race" on June 17, 2018).

71 **lose their jobs in layoffs:** According to the *New York Times* ("Layoff Rate at 8.7%, Highest Since 80's," August 2, 2004).

71 **$6.6 billion on buybacks:** From the *New York Times* ("In Yahoo, Another Example of the Buyback Mirage," March 25, 2016).

71 **more than $6 billion:** From CNN ("How Sears Wasted $6 Billion That Could Have Kept It out of Bankruptcy," October 30, 2018).

72 **just 8 percent of stocks:** From NPR ("While Trump Touts Stock
Market, Many Americans Are Left Out of the Conversation,"
March 1, 2017).

73 **"not in my business":** As reported by Axios ("Forget About Broad-
Based Pay Raises, Executives Say," May 27, 2018) at the Federal
Reserve Bank of Dallas event "Technology-Enabled Disruption:
Implications for Business, Labor Markets, and Monetary Policy"
on May 24–25, 2018.

73 **Lazonick has put it:** Lazonick's characterization of buybacks as
"profits without prosperity" was in *Harvard Business Review*
("Profits Without Prosperity," September 2014).

74 **universal basic income:** Two recommended books to learn more
about universal basic income: Rutger Bregman's *Utopia for Realists*
and Annie Lowrey's *Give People Money*.

74 **debt to enter the workforce:** Background and stats on student
loans come from CNBC ("Why Does a College Degree Cost So
Much?" in 2015 and "Student Loan Balances Jump Nearly 150 Percent in a Decade" in 2017).

76 **elections are decided almost entirely by money:** The 2015 report
on the relationship between campaign expenditures and campaign
results ("How Money Drives US Congressional Elections: More Evidence") was written by Thomas Ferguson, Paul Jorgensen, and Jie
Chen and published by the Institute for New Economic Thinking.

77 **allowed them in 1982:** Stock buyback rules were changed in 1982
when the Securities and Exchange Commission passed rule 10b-18,
which defined a process by which buybacks could legally occur.

77 **branches in multiple states:** The deregulation of banks in multiple states happened in 1994 with the Riegle-Neal Interstate Banking and Branching Efficiency Act.

78 **within a decade of their passing:** The major bill deregulating the
banking industry was the Gramm-Leach-Bliley Act in 1999.

80 **investments were made:** According to US budget data and analysis by the American Association for the Advancement of Science,
from 1970 to 2016, R&D investment as a percentage of the federal
budget declined from almost 4 percent to less than 2 percent.

82 **Ralph Gomory observes:** Ralph Gomory's observations about the Business Roundtable's Statements of Corporate Responsibility are part of his work documenting the Maximizing Class more generally. He hosts on his website the PDFs of all the Business Roundtable's previous statements (http://www.ralphgomory.com).

82 **"production distribution activities":** From *The Value of Everything* by Mariana Mazzucato (page 160).

84 **executive compensation has soared 1,000 percent:** Statistic on the 1,000 percent rise in executive compensation comes from *Bloomberg Businessweek* ("American CEO Pay Is Soaring, but the Gender Pay Gap Is Drawing the Rage," August 2018).

CHAPTER FIVE: THE TRAP

87 **It was *Harvard Business Review*:** The *Harvard Business Review* cover is from October 2015.

89 **attitudes of America's college students:** UCLA's Higher Education Research Institute's CIRP Freshman Survey reports, going all the way back to 1966 to today, can be found online at https://heri.ucla.edu/publications-tfs/.

92 **"has risen since":** This comes from Mariana Mazzucato's *The Value of Everything* (page 167).

92 **"the order of society":** This quote comes from the third chapter of another landmark work of Adam Smith, *The Theory of Moral Sentiments*, published in 1759.

94 **how they felt about them:** The study on life goals is "The Path Taken: Consequences of Attaining Intrinsic and Extrinsic Aspirations in Post-College Life" by Christopher P. Niemiec, Richard M. Ryan, and Edward L. Deci (2009). Another paper, by Tim Kasser and Richard M. Ryan, found that as people focused on extrinsic values (status, money, etc.) rather than intrinsic values (self-acceptance, belonging, community connection), the more unhappy they were ("Further Examining the American Dream: Differential Correlates of Intrinsic and Extrinsic Goals," March 1996).

95 **"recent Silicon Valley history":** The *New York Times* story about Zenefits ran on September 20, 2014.

96 **pushing for faster growth:** Eighteen months later, the *New York Times* profiled Zenefits' downfall as well ("Zenefits Scandal Highlights Perils of Hypergrowth at Start-Ups," February 17, 2016).

97 **"it does seem like a rational decision":** Andrew Mason's comments about Groupon were reported by *New York Magazine* ("The Super-Quick Rise and Even Faster Fall of Groupon," October 2018).

98 **"pound of flesh":** From *Wired* ("Waymo v. Uber Kicks Off with Travis Kalanick in the Crosshairs," February 5, 2018).

98 **role in election interference:** From the *New York Times* ("Delay, Deny, Deflect: How Facebook's Leaders Fought Through Crisis," November 14, 2018).

101 **"Only under such conditions will businesses and factories truly prosper":** Konosuke Matsushita quotes are from the book *Not for Bread Alone.*

102 **have five-day workweeks:** Details on Panasonic's change to a five-day workweek come from Panasonic's official corporate history. Information on the labor standards in Japan comes from S. J. Kim, my father-in-law, who researched this topic in Japan on my behalf.

CHAPTER SIX: WHAT'S REALLY VALUABLE?

109 **ten wealthiest people in the world:** According to *Forbes*'s 2019 list of billionaires.

110 **can't afford these things each month:** According to a 2018 study by the United Way ALICE Project ("51 Million U.S. Households Can't Afford Basics," May 17, 2018). The report states, "Some 50.8 million households or 43% of households can't afford a basic monthly budget for housing, food, transportation, child care, health care, and a monthly smartphone bill, according to an analysis of U.S. government data."

110 **long-term oriented:** For example, according to a US Census Bureau report, people coming from families in the top 25 percent in income are eight times more likely to get a college degree as ones

NOTES

from the bottom 25 percent ("Income and Poverty in the United States: 2014," September 2015).

112 **very different from today:** An eighty-nine-year-old friend of mine named Noel Osheroff (who was thirteen when Maslow's paper was published) told me she was brought up believing that people who had money or cared about money were low class. It showed they didn't have a good sense of what mattered in life. Their values were off. In her memory, this was the general attitude of most people up until the 1980s or so, when attitudes began to change.

113 **emotional well-being and income:** The paper that revealed the $75,000 threshold is "High Income Improves Evaluation of Life but Not Emotional Well-Being" by Daniel Kahneman and Angus Deaton, published in the September 2010 issue of the *Proceedings of the National Academy of Sciences of the United States of America*. As individuals made more money, their emotional well-being increased to a certain point. After that, however, researchers found that their emotional well-being grew at a much slower rate.

114 **one for every 104,000 people:** Here's the math on Jeff Bezos's personal police force if security were distributed like income. All data is current as of February 2019.

Total net worth of United States: $123.8 trillion

Total wealth of top 1%: $33.4 trillion

Total wealth of Jeff Bezos: $135 billion

Total wealth of bottom 50%: $250 billion

Applying these ratios to law enforcement numbers in America:

Total number of law enforcement officers in United States: 775,000 (as found in online estimates)

Total law enforcement officers for top 1%: 209,087

Total law enforcement officers for Jeff Bezos: 845 cops

Total law enforcement for bottom 50%: 1,565 cops for 163 million people (1 cop for every 104,000 people)

117 **study at Carnegie Mellon in 1969:** The experiment was conducted by Edward Deci, the same researcher behind the college student life goal study that surveyed students after graduation. The paper describing the experiment is called "Effects of Externally Mediated Rewards on Intrinsic Motivation," and it was published in the *Journal of Personality and Social Psychology* in 1971.

119 **our potential will grow:** There's a passage from *Drive* that I've thought about ever since reading it. Daniel Pink profiles psychologist Mihaly Csikszentmihalyi, author of the book *Flow*. He writes:

> Several years ago—he can't recall exactly when—Csikszentmihalyi was invited to Davos, Switzerland, by Klaus Schwab, who runs an annual conclave of the global power elite in that city. Joining him on the trip were three other University of Chicago faculty members—Gary Becker, George Stigler, and Milton Friedman—all of them economists, all of them winners of the Nobel Prize. The five men gathered for dinner one night and at the end of the meal, Schwab asked the academics what they considered the most important issue in modern economics.
>
> "To my incredulous surprise," Csikszentmihalyi recounted, "Becker, Stigler, and Friedman all ended up saying a variation of 'There's something missing,'" that for all its explanatory power, economics still failed to offer a rich enough account of behavior, even in business settings.

120 **"as defined above":** As Kuznets presented to Congress: "National Income, 1929–1932," 73rd US Congress, 2nd session, Senate document no. 124, page 5, 1934.

121 **It's about how much, not why:** Background on GDP came from Mariana Mazzucato's book *The Value of Everything*.

123 **cleaning another person's house is valuable:** According to a McKinsey Global Institute estimate cited in Annie Lowrey's book *Give People Money*.

124 **"measure what matters":** The title of a book by venture capitalist John Doerr.

CHAPTER SEVEN: BENTOISM

134 **"according to their nature":** The Aristotle quote on value is from *Nicomachean Ethics.*

138 **"worth going back for":** The shooting script for Quentin Tarantino's *Pulp Fiction* was found on a German fansite: pulpfiction.de.

143 **better than the one before:** With the exceptions of *Magical Mystery Tour*, *The White Album*, and *Let It Be.*

146 **They couldn't find it:** Details on the assassination of President Garfield come from "The Stalking of the President" by Gilbert King in *Smithsonian* magazine, as well as information reported by Sarah Vowell in her book *Assassination Vacation.*

147 **medicine was a routinely terrible thing:** When I say "medicine," I'm referring to Western medicine. Information on its history comes from several sources, including *Bad Medicine: Doctors Doing Harm Since Hippocrates* by historian David Wootton, which was invaluable for illuminating the long dark age of medicine, and *The Emperor of All Maladies* by Siddhartha Mukherjee, which was excellent for setting the larger context on the history of medicine generally and cancer specifically.

149 **died from postsurgical infections:** Details on Ignaz Semmelweis, Joseph Lister, and that era came from *The Doctors' Plague: Germs, Childbed Fever, and the Strange Story of Ignaz Semmelweis* by Sherwin B. Nuland, and from *Bad Medicine* by David Wootton.

150 **doubled in the twentieth century:** According to the Centers for Disease Control and Prevention's *Morbidity and Mortality Weekly Report* ("Achievements in Public Health, 1900–1999: Healthier Mothers and Babies," October 1, 1999).

150 **"fantasy of a science":** In Wootton's *Bad Medicine.*

153 **It's a competitive advantage:** For more on the philosophical roots of Bentoism, the appendix includes an essay called "The Origins of Bentoism."

CHAPTER EIGHT: ADELE GOES ON TOUR

155 **"living some mad life":** Adele's quote comes from a December 11, 2015, interview on the Norwegian-Swedish talk show *Scavlan*.

156 **shift from values to value changed our perspective:** Information on industry opinions on ticket scalping comes from *Rolling Stone* ("Is Ticketmaster's New Resale Program Helping or Hurting Fans?," May 27, 2014).

156 **in exchange for extra fees:** The Canadian Broadcasting Corporation ("'I'm Getting Ripped Off': A Look Inside Ticketmaster's Price-Hiking Bag of Tricks," September 18, 2018).

156 **are doing the selling:** The *Wall Street Journal* ("Concert Tickets Get Set Aside, Marked Up by Artists, Managers," March 2009).

157 **"go to one show":** Information on industry opinions on ticket scalping comes from *Rolling Stone* ("Is Ticketmaster's New Resale Program Helping or Hurting Fans?," May 27, 2014).

158 **rather than through scalpers:** Information about the collaboration and Adele fans saving $6.5 million in ticket prices comes from *The Atlantic* ("Adele Versus the Scalpers," December 25, 2015).

160 **score more points in the long run:** The chart that analyzed shot quality in the NBA comes from a paper titled "Quantifying Shot Quality in the NBA" by Yu-Han Chang, cofounder of Second Spectrum, a service that provides detailed analytics to NBA teams and writers. The paper was published in 2014 as part of MIT's Sloan Sports Analytics Conference. Other key figures in this movement included John Hollinger, Kirk Goldsberry, Martin Manley, and Daryl Morey.

162 **pressured other artists not to follow her lead:** Later that year, Songkick filed a federal antitrust lawsuit against Live Nation alleging that the ticketing behemoth used unfair practices against Songkick, including threatening to ban artists who used its new tool from performing at Live Nation–owned venues. Live Nation settled the case, paying Songkick $110 million and acquiring the patents to Songkick's technology. Sources: *New York Times* ("Songkick Sues Live Nation, Saying It Abuses Its Market Power," December 22, 2015), *Wall Street Journal* ("Songkick Suing Live Nation,

Ticketmaster," December 22, 2015), and *New York Times* ("Live Nation Settles Suit with Ticketing Startup, Buying Its Assets," January 12, 2018).

165 **highly rated fast-food chain:** Chick-fil-A was named the highest-rated fast-food restaurant in the 2018 American Customer Satisfaction Index.

165 **$1 billion a year:** The estimate of Chick-fil-A's losses from being closed on Sunday comes from a calculation done by a Quora user, Maxwell Arnold, based on the company's annual sales.

167 **"purse upgrades":** *Mr. Money Mustache*'s passionate pitch for FIRE comes from a February 22, 2013, blog post titled "Getting Rich: From Zero to Hero in One Blog Post."

167 **"upscale lifestyle":** The quotes about the woman who sold her BMW and the person living below his or her means come from the *New York Times* ("How to Retire in Your 30s with $1 Million in the Bank," September 1, 2018).

170 **legally backed demands:** The complicated fate of Ben & Jerry's is well covered in the book *Ice Cream Social: The Struggle for the Soul of Ben & Jerry's* by Brad Edmondson, and by the *New York Times*, which quoted one of the company's investors: "We think it's horrible that a company has no choice but to sell to the highest bidder or get sued" ("Ben & Jerry's to Unilever, with Attitude," April 13, 2000).

170 **company's legal foundation:** Jay Coen Gilbert, Andrew Kassoy, and Bart Houlahan are responsible for creating the public benefit corporation movement in the United States. This work began in 2007, when the three left their jobs in private equity to advocate for a new corporate category that would focus on long-term value creation. By 2010, the first US state legalized this new structure. As of 2018, thirty-five states now permit PBCs. Kickstarter, Patagonia, Method, and others are among the organizations that have benefited from their work to bridge the value gap.

170 **end systemic inequality:** Kickstarter's full public benefit charter can be found online: https://www.kickstarter.com/charter.

170 **website called The Creative Independent:** The Creative Independent can be found online at http://www.thecreativeindependent.com.

172 *People Go Surfing*: Information on Patagonia's repair program came from the company's website and *Fast Company* ("Don't Throw That Jacket Away; Patagonia Is Taking Its Worn Wear Program on the Road," April 2015). Details on Patagonia's corporate policies come from *Let My People Go Surfing* by Yvon Chouinard.

172 **"positive impact on the environment"**: Patagonia's public benefit statements can be found at https://www.patagonia.com/b-lab.html.

172 **"we're giving it away"**: The biorubber story comes from a report by Sustainable Brands ("Patagonia Sharing Proprietary Biorubber to Advance Sustainable Surf Industry").

173 **"factories every day"**: Elon Musk's blog post announcing Tesla's new patent policy was titled "All Our Patent Are Belong to You," June 12, 2014 (https://www.tesla.com/blog/all-our-patent-are-belong-you).

CHAPTER NINE: HOW TO DO A PERFECT HANDSTAND

180 **thirty years as a cadence for change**: My thinking on the thirty-year theory of change was first sparked by Thomas Piketty's *Capital in the Twenty-First Century*. In particular, his demonstration of the impact of a 1 percent growth rate over the course of thirty years. Using basic accounting and money management practices, Piketty shows how a small amount of change accelerates over time. I wondered, *Is this what's happening around us?* As I started looking at the world through this lens, I began to believe that change was like Piketty's capital growth rates. Exercise, recycling, organic food, opinions on gay marriage, the growth of financial maximization, and even hip-hop were all movements that began as something tiny. But thirty years later, they had become new normals, with the final stages of growth being quite rapid.

181 **is a continuous process**: From Mannheim's essay "The Problem of Generations," which also alludes to thirty years as a meaningful rate of change. As does the early-twentieth-century Spanish philosopher José Ortega y Gasset, who says change takes fifteen years of preparing and fifteen years of acting. (This according to *Generations: A Historical Method*, a book by his protégé Julián Marías, in

1970.) The French philosopher Auguste Comte does as well, in the collection of his nineteenth-century writings *The Positive Philosophy and the Study of Society*, which finds evidence of numerous, significant thirty-year changes in France's history. A master's thesis by Sharon Opal Scully titled "The Theory of Generational Change: A Critical Reassessment" was a helpful overview.

182 **fresh arrivals learn the ropes:** We imagine a world with longer life spans as a more peaceful and idyllic world. It could be the opposite. A world with longer life spans is one where the dance floor is more crowded. The in-power generation would no longer have the hard stop of imminent death to remove them from the dance floor. This could lead to societies becoming more conservative, with aging generations holding on to power longer, and younger generations' influence diminishing.

182 **4.3 people are born:** Birth and death rates come from the CIA's *World Factbook*.

182 **the larger population will be new:** This assertion is based on US Census projections ("Projections of the Size and Composition of the U.S. Population: 2014 to 2060," March 2015).

184 **his methods outlasted his critics:** Information on Joseph Lister's treatment of the incoming king of England comes from the blog Cemetery Club, run by a City of Westminster guide named Sheldon K. Goodman ("The Man Who Saved a King," February 29, 2016), as well as from a paper by Ulrich Tröhler, "Statistics and the British Controversy About the Effects of Joseph Lister's System of Antisepsis for Surgery, 1867–1890," in the *Journal of the Royal Society of Medicine*, July 2015.

184 **new becomes normal:** Thirty years as a meaningful time frame for change is also supported through a line of thought called "cycle theories." These are theories of repeating patterns—whether they're economic, social, or other historical behaviors—in human history.

For example, the historian Arthur Schlesinger Sr. theorized that political power shifts from left to right and vice versa every fifteen years. Conservatives are in power for fifteen years before progressives counter with fifteen years of their own power. "Each generation spends its first fifteen years after coming of political age in challenging the generation already entrenched in power," he writes. "Then the new generation comes to power itself for another fifteen years, after which its policies pale and the generation coming up behind claims the succession."

Schlesinger wrote this in 1939 in an essay titled "Tides of American Politics." He charted this model backward and forward in time with remarkable accuracy. His model identified the New Deal and predicted the progressive 1960s and the conservative 1980s. His theory also predicted fifteen years of progressive rule starting in 1990. Which means that the *Bush v. Gore* Supreme Court decision broke the matrix and caused the havoc that has been the world ever since. Had Gore won in 2000, the Iraq War would not have happened, which means the mass displacement of people in the Middle East would not have happened, and Trump and Brexit probably wouldn't have happened. But I digress.

There are longer cyclical theories as well. The economist Joseph Schumpeter was fascinated with what he called "long-wave theory"—a pattern of economic growth and contraction with an interval of sixty years. They are called Kondratiev waves, named after the Soviet economist who first observed them. Schumpeter and other economists found evidence of Kondratiev waves coinciding with major innovations, from industrialization to the automobile to the internet. In these instances, thirty years of infrastructure building happened first—like the construction of the railroads—then a second thirty-year boom happened as that new technology was utilized. The internet is another example of this.

What's most interesting about Schumpeter's theory is *when* the technological breakthroughs happen. They don't happen in the good times. They happen in lean times. The theory being that when there's not as much easy money to be made, people invest in riskier, longer-term things. We look to the other areas out of desperation and necessity. When we do, we find opportunity.

The optimist's argument for exercise, organic food, and recycling would be that these are also Kondratiev wave–like trends. The first thirty years were spent creating the infrastructure and doing normal science. The next thirty years will be spent getting those behaviors to full capacity as the new norms.

Two other important sources of background on this area are Thomas Kuhn's book *The Structure of Scientific Revolutions* and J. Z. Young's book *Doubt and Certainty in Science*. Kuhn's book is tremendous in its description of how paradigms and "normal science"—the process by which we test and build out a new way of seeing—create new approaches to knowledge. J. Z. Young, a biologist, explains in vivid and compelling detail how our brains learn and acquire new knowledge. The neurological background for why we are the way we are.

185 **"The Soft American":** John F. Kennedy's *Sports Illustrated* article "The Soft American" was published on December 26, 1960.

185 **history of exercise:** From Harold Zinkin's memoir *Remembering Muscle Beach: Where Hard Bodies Began.*

186 **weight lifting in the 1960s:** Arnold Schwarzenegger's CNN editorial ("How I Fought My Way Back to Fitness," December 2018).

186 **running in 1968:** The story of Strom Thurmond being arrested while jogging and the growing trend of jogging comes from a *Vox* article ("When Running for Exercise Was for Weirdos," August 9, 2015).

186 **ten times that many:** From the paper "The Fitness Movement and the Fitness Center Industry, 1960–2000" by Marc Stern.

189 **a beverage executive said in 2000:** The quote about bottled water is Susan Wellington's, then president of the Quaker Oats Company's United States beverage division, as recounted in the book *Bottled and Sold: The Story Behind Our Obsession with Bottled Water* by Peter H. Gleick.

190 **depressing exuberance:** The story of London adding new drinking fountains was found in the *Guardian* ("First of London's New Drinking Fountains Revealed," March 25, 2018).

191 **harder to come by:** One might counter by saying, What about Trump? Or Brexit? Aren't those examples of instant, visible results? Absolutely. But I also think some of those are violent changes. Changes implemented *upon* people, rather than negotiated among

people over the course of time. This is *not* the kind of change we
need.

192 **this was thirty-five years away:** Isaac Asimov's predictions of the
future were published in the Canadian newspaper the *Star* ("35
Years Ago, Isaac Asimov Was Asked by the *Star* to Predict the
World of 2019. Here Is What He Wrote," December 27, 2018).

CHAPTER TEN: VALUES MAXIMIZING CLASS

195 **"economic necessity into daylight":** John Maynard Keynes's
words about the nature of capitalism come from the 1930 essay
"Economic Possibilities for Our Grandchildren," collected in a
book of Keynes's writings called *Essays in Persuasion*.

196 **271 times more than the average worker:** From *Fortune* ("CEO
Pay: Top Execs Make 271 Times More Than Workers," July 20,
2017).

196 **seventeenth in 2018:** From *U.S. News & World Report* ("Quality of
Life" 2018 ratings).

198 **Chile's Atacama Desert:** Background on the Chilean miner
story came from NPR ("The Incredible Story of Chilean Miners
Rescued from the 'Deep Down Dark,'" October 29, 2014); the
book *Deep Down Dark* by Héctor Tobar; and a Harvard Business
School case study ("The 2010 Chilean Mining Rescue," October 2014 by Amy C. Edmondson, Faaiza Rashid, and Herman
"Dutch" Leonard).

199 **found the way to live:** Another notable exploration of the tension
between our individual and collective responsibilities comes from
a highly recommended book called *Small Is Beautiful* by E. F.
Schumacher. He writes:

> Nowhere is this dichotomy [between the individual and col-
> lective] more noticeable than in connection with the use of
> land. The farmer is considered simply as a producer who must
> cut his costs and raise his efficiency by every possible device,
> even if he thereby destroys—for man-as-consumer—the

health of the soil and the beauty of the landscape, and even if the end effect is the depopulation of the land and the over-crowding of cities. There are large-scale farmers, horticultur-alists, food manufacturers and food growers today who would never think of consuming any of their own products. "Luck-ily," they say, "we have enough money to be able to afford to buy products which have been organically grown, without the use of poisons." When they are asked why they themselves do not adhere to organic methods and avoid the use of poisonous substances, they reply that they could not afford to do so. What man-as-producer can afford is one thing; what man-as-consumer can afford is quite another thing. But since the two are the same man, the question of what man—or society—can really afford gives rise to endless confusion.

Another compelling line of thought on this comes from the film-maker Adam Curtis in an interview I did with him for The Creative Independent ("Adam Curtis on the Dangers of Self-Expression," March 14, 2017):

If you want to make the world a better place, you have to start with where power has gone. It's very difficult to see. We live in a world where we see ourselves as independent individuals. If you're an independent individual, you don't really think in terms of power. You think only in terms of your own influence on the world.

What you don't see is what people in the past were more able to see. When you are in groups, you can be very powerful. You can change things. You have confidence when things go wrong that you don't when you're on your own. That's why the whole concept of power has dwindled. We're encouraged just to talk about ourselves and our feelings towards others. We're not encouraged to see ourselves as part of anything.

But the computers know the truth. They see us as a group. We're actually quite similar to each other. We have the same desires, ambitions, and fears. Computers spot this through correlations and patterns.

Computers can see us as large groups, but they're glum and only aggregate us to sell us stuff. In reality, the computers give great insight into the power of common identity among groups. No one's using that. What's sitting with the computers is a way of seeing new groups, and new common identities between people.

201 **piece of paper:** For a guided experience to create your own Bento, visit: https://www.ystrickler.com/bento.

212 **"secular mission to the world":** From Konosuke Matsushita's book *Not for Bread Alone.*

214 **the second floor:** The idea that banks would be on the second floor in 2050 is inspired by a woman named Gale Brewer. In 2012 as a New York City councilwoman she introduced a zoning change limiting the amount of storefront space banks could use in the Upper East Side of Manhattan, the area she represented. This resulted in banks having smaller entrances on the streets and branches on the second floor of buildings instead of the ground floor. An inspired and simple solution.

223 **without generational influence:** David Hume wrote "Of the Original Contract" in 1752. I discovered Hume's experiment in Karl Mannheim's essay "The Problem of Generations." Mannheim writes:

> Suppose, [Hume] said, the type of succession of human generations to be completely altered to resemble that of a butterfly or caterpillar, so that the older generation disappears at one stroke and the new one is born all at once. Further, suppose man to be of such a high degree of mental development as to be capable of choosing rationally the form of government most suitable for himself. (This, of course, was the main problem of Hume's time.) These conditions given, he said, it would be both possible and proper for each generation, without reference to

the ways of its ancestors, to choose afresh its own particular form of state. Only because mankind is as it is—generation following generation in a continuous stream, so that whenever one person dies off, another is born to replace him—do we find it necessary to preserve the continuity of our forms of government. Hume thus translates the principle of political continuity into terms of the biological continuity of generations.

INDEX

AUTHOR BIOGRAPHY

Yancey Strickler is a writer and the cofounder and former CEO of Kickstarter. He grew up in Clover Hollow, Virginia, and began his career as a music critic in New York City. This is his first book.